Distinctive Vegetarian Cuisine

Lively & Appetizing Vegan Cookery

By Sue M. Weir

Distinctive Vegetarian Cuisine
Lively & Appetizing Vegan Cookery
By Sue M. Weir

A Weir Writings Publication / March , 1995

Copyright © 1995
by Sue M. Weir
All rights reserved.

This book may not be reproduced without permission in whole or in part, by means, electronic or mechanical, except for short quotations to be used in reviews. For information write to, Weir Writings, P.O. Box 10497, Spokane, WA 99209

Book and cover design by Edward Weir
Manufactured in the UNITED STATES OF AMERICA

First Edition

ISBN 0-9645579-0-8

FOREWORD

Distinctive Vegetarian Cuisine is a pure vegetarian cookbook. The recipes contain no meat, dairy products, eggs, cheese, or honey.

My deepest appreciation and gratitude to my husband, Eddie, who spent many hours at the computer learning how to use the programs necessary to put this book together. I also thank him for encouraging me to get this book finished and printed. Thank you to Dr. Agatha Thrash for the educational information, recipes, and support. Thank you to other family members and friends for your recipes that help make up this book. And thank you to those who tasted as I tested!

This book is dedicated to all of those wishing to eat HEALTHY foods, but not wanting to give up DELICIOUS tasting foods. Vegetarian cooking does not have to be bland, tasteless, and unappealing, as you will find out as you begin to cook these meals. Be creative when preparing and serving your meals. Make it appealing to the smell, sight, and taste. And most of all, ENJOY!

CONTENTS

Breads	1
Breakfasts	29
Nondairy milks	57
Entree's	71
Gravies and Sauces	155
Cheeses, Spreads, and Condiments	171
Vegetables	195
Soups	221
Salads	241
Salad Dressings	259
Desserts	269
Four Week Meal Planner	303
Index	317

TWO MEAL PLAN

Most people do better on two meals a day than on three. Careful attention to proper rest for the stomach lessens the likelihood of getting ulcers or gastritis. Since the digestive apparatus requires 5 or more hours to digest a meal, assimilate it, and get recharged for the next meal, it is taxing to the body's economy to crowd three meals into the stomach. No food should ever be eaten within several hours of going to bed, as recuperation from fatigue is seriously impaired if digestion is going on. The wisest plan is to take a large breakfast, a generous dinner, and no supper. Dinner can be taken in the mid-afternoon so that the appetite for supper is eliminated. If no evening food is taken, a good appetite for breakfast will gradually develop. Studies show that we need this meal more than any other. It gets all the biochemical systems supplied with raw materials. Make it a good one.

If a third meal is taken it should be light. Fruit and toast or plain crackers serves best as they are most promptly digested. Oils, nuts, and other fatty foods remain in the stomach much longer, and are unsuitable for supper.

IS YOUR FOOD PALATABLE?

The following errors can make your food unpalatable:

1. Cooking too long
2. Undercooking
3. Stirring too much
4. Too salty
5. Not enough salt
6. Too sweet
7. Not sweet enough
8. Scorching
9. Not thick enough (in puddings)
10. Too thick (in gravies and sauces)
11. Not enough seasoning
12. Too much seasoning
13. Using the same seasoning in several dishes at the same meal

IS YOUR FOOD ATTRACTIVE

Foods are unattractive when too little color is used at the same meal, such as:

Cashew Rice Loaf	White
Cashew Gravy	White
Wax Beans	Yellow
Cucumber Slices	White
White bread	White
Lemon Pie	Yellow

Foods are unattractive when too many colors are used at the same meal, such as:

Greens	Green
Beets	Purplish Red
Sweet Potatoes	Orange
Tomatoes	Red
Kidney beans	Maroon
Creamed Corn	Yellow
Whole wheat bread	Brown

Foods may appear unattractive also if the following are present at your table:

1. Linens are soiled or poorly ironed
2. The table is too large
3. The table is too small
4. Broken dishes are used
5. Kitchen utensils are used, rather than serving utensils
6. Silverware is stained
7. The table is carelessly set
8. Too many decorations are on the table
9. No centerpiece
10. Foods are placed on the table in the containers in which they were purchased at the store, such as:

    Cereal box
    Box of raisins
    Syrup in bottle
    Peanut butter in jar
    Bread in wrapper

MAKING FOODS ATTRACTIVE

Set the table with an attractive center piece, such as a bowl of luscious fruit, a pretty potted plant, or a low bowl of beautiful flowers.

The colors red, green, golden brown, yellow, cream, pink, and tan are colors that stimulate the appetite.

Add chopped parsley to boiled potatoes.

Sprinkle chopped chives or green onions over mashed potatoes.

Tuck sprigs of parsley here and there on loaves and casseroles.

Add a sprig of mint to lemonade.

Place a few lovely flowers among plain looking cookies.

Place a few strips of pimento on lettuce topped with mayonnaise.

Place a bright red cherry atop white puddings.

Sprinkle chopped nuts on whipped cream toppings or puddings.

Add peppers or pimentos to macaroni or potato salads.

Be creative when arranging foods on serving platters.

Slices of tomatoes enhance the appearance of colorless foods served on platters.

SERVE FOODS IN A VARIETY OF WAYS

Foods grow unpalatable when they are served in the same way every time.

Peas may be served creamed, in soups, in salads, in loafs, or on toast.

Beans may be served baked with molasses or tomato sauce, in soups, baked in loafs or patties, added to salads, or mashed for sandwich spreads.

Potatoes may be served baked, browned, boiled, mashed and topped with gravy, creamed, scalloped, in salads, or in soups.

Vegetables may be cooked with onions, garlic, or tomato sauce. They can be served in a white sauce. They can be scalloped or cooked in a casserole. They can be added to salads.

Juicy foods may be served in a pastry cup or over a piece of toast.

Fresh fruits may be served plain, or in salads.

Cooked fruits may be served in sauce, fruit soup, puddings, cobblers, pies, crisps, or added to cooked cereals.

DOES YOUR COOKING TASTE FLAT?

Below are a few suggestions to add flavor to your foods:

1. Add onions to foods that are to flat. For those who dislike onions, use a few drops of onion juice. Rub an onion on a grater for juice.

2. Sauteed tomatoes, onions and green peppers added to corn, string beans, okra, eggplant, and greens give them zest. Try this when you grow tired of them plain.

3. A hint of garlic is almost indispensable in green salads. Since garlic is strongly flavored, use it sparingly.

4. Dextrinized flour adds wonderful flavor to gravies. Sift flour onto cookie sheet, dry in a slow oven, then turn up heat and brown to a tan color. Stir often to prevent burning the flour.

5. Chopped parsley is a must with stewed onions or potatoes.

FOOD STORAGE

Use the freezer for long-term storage and keep it set at 0 degrees or lower. It is best to thaw frozen foods in the refrigerator, in a microwave, or in a sealed bag under cold running water.

For perishable foods that are to be used within a few days, use the refrigerator for storage. Keep refrigerator temperature between 36 degrees F. and 40 degrees F.

Store canned goods in a cool, dry, well ventilated place away from sunlight, between 50 degrees F. and 70 degrees F.

Store flour, sugar, and dried legumes in covered containers in the freezer to retain freshness.

Cover and chill, or freeze cooled foods and leftovers promptly. Use moisture-vapor proof materials such as freezer paper or heavy foil, or freezer containers for freezing.

Store fresh fruits and vegetables in the refrigerator crisper. Keep potatoes and onions in a cool, well ventilated place.

VITAMIN SOURCES

A   Green and yellow vegetables and fruits.

B_1 (Thiamine) Whole grains, legumes, nuts, greens.

B_2 (Riboflavin) Greens, wheat, vegetables.

B_3 (Niacin) Whole grains, nuts.

B_6 (Pyridoxine) Wheat, nuts, legumes, cabbage, bananas.
(Pantothenic acid) Legumes, wheat.
(Biotin) Legumes.
(Folic acid) Green vegetables, wheat.
(Choline) Whole grains.

C   Greens, peppers, citrus fruits, cabbage, tomatoes, potatoes.

D   Sunshine: A fair-skinned person needs only a 6" square of skin exposed daily to the sun for 1 hour. The darker the skin the longer the exposure needed.

E   Vegetable oils, whole grains, vegetables.

K   Cabbage, cauliflower, spinach.

Breads

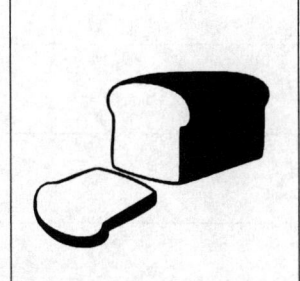

BREADS

Apple-Date Muffins	19
Banana Bran Muffins	21
Banana Bread	20
Blueberry Muffins	17
Bread Rolls	13
Breading Meal	27
Coconut Chews	26
Coriander Rolls	22
Corn Bread	14
Croutons	27
Garlic Bread Chips	26
Garlic Toast	24
Hush Puppies	23
Oat Bread	15

Oat Crackers	23
Oat Gems	24
One Loaf Recipe for Children	12
Raisin Bread	18
Rye Bread	16
Sesame Crackers	25
Tortillas	25
White Bread	11
Whole Wheat Bread	10

Chapter One

YEAST BREADS

When making bread you will want your loaves to look and taste wonderful. Below are some helpful hints for achieving excellence.

Do not start a batch of bread until you have read the recipe all the way through, know that you have the proper ingredients, and understand the mixing method.

If you are just learning to bake, try a simple basic recipe first, such as WHITE BREAD.

Use only the freshest and best quality of flours. Old flour may not rise. The high gluten content of hard wheat flour makes it best for bread making. A mixture of two or three flours is quite nutritious. Breads made from mixtures of two or three grains should be used alternately with single grain breads for best nutrition. To avoid a "complex mixture," do not mix a large number of grains in one loaf.

When the recipe gives a range on the amount of flour, start by adding the smaller amount. Remember that the flour used in kneading is part of the measured amount.

Develop the gluten of wheat flour in the batter by beating thoroughly or squeezing between fingers before adding other flours which have no gluten. Gluten toughens on beating, enabling it to hold air bubbles better.

When the dough is ready to mold into loaves, grease your hands and the pans well with solid shortening (oil will cause sticking). Form the dough into a smooth ball or loaf, and tuck it is so that the edges touch the sides of the pan, snugly and smoothly.

Do not place dough in a hot area to rise, excessive heat will kill the yeast. A good spot to rise bread is in an unheated oven with a large pan of hot water set on the lower rack under the bowl of dough. The optimum rising temperature is about 80 degrees.

Do not add flour after rising starts.

Do not let loaves rise too long or to the top of the pan.

When baking the loaves the temperature should not be so hot as to overcook the outside of the loaf before the inside is cooked. Preheat the oven for 5 minutes at 400 degrees. The bread will rise for the first 10 minutes and by then will have sufficient crust to hold it firm. Loaves need to be small enough that the loaf may be well baked in 45 minutes. A well baked loaf may be lifted from the pan and placed on the palm without burning it, as the moisture is evaporated. Yeast bread should be "light and dry". "Light" is a word having to do with the bubbles made in the dough, and not to the weight of the loaf.

Before baking brush the top of the loaf with vegetable shortening or oil for a browner crust. Brush with soy milk, or water for a shiny crust. For a softer crust, brush the top with margarine after baking.

Flours grow stale and rancid on aging. For this reason it is well to keep all grains, whether whole or ground, refrigerated or frozen during storage.

Chapter One

COMMON DEFECTS OF BREAD AND POSSIBLE CAUSES

1. ## SOUR TASTE

    a. Water too warm.
    b. Period of rising too long, especially in whole grain breads which will not rise as light as white breads.
    c. Temperature too high while rising.
    d. Poor yeast.

2. ## DRY OR CRUMBLY

    a. Too much flour in dough.
    b. Overbaking.

3. ## HEAVINESS

    a. Unevenness of temperature while rising.
    b. Insufficient kneading.
    c. Old flour.
    d. Old yeast.

4. ## CRACKS IN CRUST

    a. Cooling in a draft.
    b. Baking before sufficiently light.
    c. Oven too hot at first.

Breads

5. TOO THICK A CRUST

    a. Oven too slow.
    b. Baked too long.
    c. Excess of salt.

6. DARK PATCHES OR STREAKS

    a. Poor materials.
    b. Shortening added to flour before liquid, thus allowing flour particles to become coated with fat before they had mixed evenly with the liquid.

7. SOGGINESS

    a. Too much liquid.
    b. Insufficient baking.
    c. Cooling in airtight container.

8. ILL-SHAPED LOAF

    a. Not molded well originally.
    b. Too large a loaf for the pan.
    c. Rising period too long.
    d. Failure to rise to greatest size in oven.
    e. Loaves flat on top may result from inadequate kneading.

Chapter One

9. COARSE GRAIN

  a. Too high temperature during rising.
  b. Rising too long or proofing too long.
  c. Oven too cool at first.
  d. Pan too large for size of loaf.
  e. Too much liquid.

BREAD BRAID

You can make one braid from a recipe based on 3 ½ to 4 cups flour.

Preparing the dough: Mix the bread dough following recipe instructions. Knead the dough and let rise until double in a warm place. Punch down. Divide the dough into thirds and shape each portion into a ball. Cover and let rest 10 minutes. On a lightly floured surface roll each ball into an evenly thick rope about 16 inches long. Line up the three ropes 1 inch apart on a oiled baking sheet.

Braiding the bread: Begin in the middle of the ropes and work toward the ends. Braid the ropes loosely so that the dough has room to expand without losing its shape. Straighten the ropes on the baking sheet. Pinch the ends of the rope together and tuck the sealed portion under so the ropes won't come lose. Cover the braid and let rise in a warm place until double. Sprinkle with sesame seed or poppy seed if desired. Bake according to recipe directions.

SHAPING DINNER ROLLS

To Make CLOVERLEAVES, lightly grease 24 muffin cups. Divide each half of dough into 36 pieces. Shape each piece of dough into a ball, pulling edges under to make a smooth top. Place 3 balls in each muffin cup, smooth side up. Let rise and bake according to directions.

To make BUTTERHORNS, lightly grease baking sheets. On a lightly floured surface roll each half of dough into 12-inch circle. Cut each circle into 12 wedges. To shape, begin at wide end of wedge and roll toward point. Place point down 2 to 3 inches apart on baking sheets. Let rise and bake according to directions.

To make PARKER HOUSE ROLLS, lightly oil baking sheets. On a lightly floured surface roll out each half of dough to 1/4 inch thickness. Cut with a floured 2 1/2 inch round cutter. Make an off-center crease in each round. Fold so large half overlaps slightly. Place 2 inches apart on baking sheets. Let rise and bake according to directions.

To make ROSETTES, lightly oil baking sheets. Divide each half of dough into 16 pieces. On a lightly floured surface roll each piece into 12-inch rope. Tie in a loose knot, leaving two long ends. Tuck top end under roll. Bring bottom end up; tuck into center of roll. Place 2 inches apart on baking sheets. Let rise and bake according to directions.

Chapter One

WHOLE WHEAT BREAD

3 cups water
3 tablespoons Karo
3 teaspoons salt
3 tablespoons vegetable oil
3 tablespoons yeast
8 cups whole wheat flour, warmed in oven for 3-5 minutes at 275 degrees

Have all ingredients warm, and work in a warm room. Mix the first four ingredients in a bowl. Add yeast and flour to the mixture in a large mixing bowl. Work together well by squeezing through fingers. Add flour if needed. Keep the dough sticky as too much flour added makes a flat loaf. As soon as the dough begins to turn loose from the fingers, oil the hands and the bowl to prevent sticking. Let rise in bowl, set in a warm place, covered, until double in bulk. Cut into 3 parts with a sharp knife and place in oiled loaf pans. Shape loaves nicely. Allow to rise until double in bulk. Place in preheated 400 degree oven for 15 minutes. Reduce heat to 350 degrees for about 30 minutes. Remove from pans and cool on wire rack.

Makes 2 loaves

WHITE BREAD

1 package dry yeast
2 tablespoons sugar
2 teaspoons salt
1/4 cups warm water
2 cups soy milk, or water
1 tablespoon vegetable shortening
5-6 cups flour

Dissolve yeast in 1/4 cup of the warm water and set aside. In a saucepan heat soy milk (or water), sugar, shortening, and salt until warm and shortening is almost melted. Place in a large mixing bowl. Stir in 2 cups of the flour, beat well. Add yeast, mix until smooth. Gradually add flour to form a soft dough. Turn onto floured surface and knead until smooth. Place in oiled bowl. Cover and let rise about 1 1/4 hours. Punch down. Divide into 2 portions and form loaves. Place in oiled bread pans. Cover with a towel and set in a warm place to rise until nearly double. Bake at 375 degrees for 25 to 30 minutes. Cool on wire racks.

Makes 2 loaves

Chapter One

ONE LOAF RECIPE FOR CHILDREN

1 cup warm water
2 tablespoons sugar
1 tablespoon yeast
1 teaspoon salt
1 tablespoon oil
2 ½ cups whole wheat flour

Mix first three ingredients and let stand 10 to 15 minutes. Add remaining ingredients and squeeze between fingers, hand over hand until all is mixed and dough begins to turn loose from fingers. May need to add more flour. Turn onto oiled board and knead well. Shape immediately into oiled loaf pan, and let rise until double. Bake at 350 degrees for 45 to 50 minutes.

Makes 1 loaf

BREAD ROLLS

2 packages dry yeast
1/2 cup warm water (about 110 degrees F)
1 cup soy milk
1 1/2 teaspoon salt
1/2 cup corn syrup
2 tablespoons vegetable oil
3 1/2 cups whole wheat flour

Dissolve the yeast in the warm water. Combine the soy milk, salt, corn syrup, and oil and heat to warm. Mix to make sure the corn syrup is completely dissolved. Stir the yeast into the soy milk mixture. Gradually add the flour, stirring with a wooden spoon. Add more or less flour to make a stiff but pliable dough. Turn the dough out onto a floured board, knead for 10 minutes, then form into a ball. Oil a large bowl and place the dough in it, smooth side down. Turn it to oil all sides. Cover with a damp cloth and set in a warm place to rise until doubled in bulk, about 45 minutes. Cut the dough into two pieces. Roll each piece out into a rectangle about 1/2 inch thick and 8 inches wide. Roll up the dough lengthwise and cut into rolls about 1 inch thick. Place with cut side down, in two oiled cake pans. Cover with a cloth and set in a warm place to rise until doubled in bulk. Preheat the oven to 400 degrees and bake for about 20 minutes.

Makes about 18 rolls

Chapter One

CORN BREAD

2 cups warm water
1 tablespoon dry yeast
¼ cup corn syrup
2 ½ cups corn meal
1 cup whole wheat flour
1 cup unbleached white flour
1 ½ teaspoons salt
¼ cup oil

In small bowl mix first three ingredients. Let stand 10 minutes. In a separate bowl, mix remaining ingredients. Combine all ingredients and mix well. Pour into oiled baking dish, and let rise in a warm place until just below top of dish (10-15 minutes). Bake at 350 degrees for 40 minutes, or until golden brown.

Breads

OAT BREAD

1 package dry yeast
½ cup warm water
1 cup quick oats
½ cup whole wheat flour
½ cup molasses
1 tablespoon salt
2 tablespoons oil
2 cups boiling water
5-6 cups white flour

Dissolve yeast in warm water. In large bowl combine oats, whole wheat flour, sugar, salt, and oil. Pour boiling water over all and mix well. When mixture is cooled to lukewarm stir in yeast. Stir in about half of the flour. Turn onto floured surface and knead in remaining flour. Place in oiled bowl. Cover and let rise until double. Punch down. Shape into two loaves and place in oiled bread pans. Let rise again until nearly double. Bake at 350 degrees for 30 to 40 minutes. Cool on rack.

Makes 2 loaves

Chapter One

RYE BREAD

1 package dry yeast
1/2 cup warm water
2 cups rye flour
3/4 cups dark molasses
1/3 cup vegetable shortening
2 teaspoons salt
2 cups boiling water
6 cups white flour

Dissolve yeast in warm water. In large bowl, combine rye flour, molasses, shortening, salt, and boiling water. Mix well. Cool to lukewarm. Add yeast mixture. Gradually add white flour to make a soft dough. Turn onto floured surface and knead well. Place dough in oiled bowl. Turn once to oil surface. Cover and let rise in warm place until doubled. Punch down in bowl. Cover and let rise again until double. Turn onto floured surface. Shape into 3 loaves and place in well oiled bread pans. Let rise again about 30 minutes. Bake at 350 degrees for 35 to 40 minutes. Remove from pans. Cool on wire racks.

Makes 2 loaves

Breads

BLUEBERRY MUFFINS

2 tablespoons dry yeast
½ cup warm water
1 tablespoon corn syrup
1 cup warm water
1 cup date sugar
1 tablespoon vanilla
1 teaspoon salt
½ cup oil
1 ½ cups whole wheat flour
2 cups fresh or frozen blueberries

Dissolve yeast and corn syrup in ½ cup warm water. Let stand for 5 minutes. Meanwhile blend 1 cup warm water, date sugar, vanilla, salt, and oil in blender. Add to yeast mixture, stir slightly. Fold in flour. Let rise 15 to 20 minutes. Fold in blueberries. If using frozen berries, thaw first by running under warm tap water, drain. Fill greased and floured muffin cups about ⅔ full. Let set for 10 minutes. Bake at 350 degrees for 35 minutes.

Chapter One

RAISIN BREAD

2 cups unsulfured raisins
1 cup apple juice
1/4 cup warm water (110 degrees F)
1 package active dry yeast
2 teaspoons salt
6 cups whole wheat flour
water
1 1/4 cups soy milk, warmed
2 tablespoons vegetable oil

Combine the raisins and apple juice in a small saucepan. Boil 1 minute and let stand until the raisins are plump. Drain and set aside. Place 1/4 cup of warm water in a small glass bowl and stir in yeast. Into a large mixing bowl, sift the salt and flour together and set aside. In a small bowl, combine the raisin liquid plus enough water to make 1 1/4 cups, the warm soy milk and oil. Stir in the yeast mixture. Pour into the center of the flour and stir until all flour is moistened. When the dough leaves the side of the mixing bowl knead it with your hands a few times. If the dough is tough and hard, sprinkle a tablespoon of water on the dough and see if it becomes pliable enough to knead. Repeat until the dough responds. If the dough is too thin, sprinkle a tablespoon of flour on it and knead a few times. Turn dough out onto a lightly floured board. Let stand covered for 5 minutes. Knead the dough until it becomes smooth and pliable and loses its stickiness. Roll the dough into a ball and place it smooth side down in a large oiled bowl. Roll it over to oil all sides. Cover with a damp towel and set in a warm place to rise until it doubles in bulk, about 1 1/2 hours. When the dough is ready, press it down again to expel the air. Push the sides down into the center and turn the dough over. Cover with a damp towel and return to a warm place and rise again for 45 minutes. Turn the dough out onto a clean board and divide into two pieces. Shape into loaves. Place in two lightly oiled loaf pans, cover with a damp cloth, and return to warm place to rise for 1 more hour. Preheat the oven to 350 degrees. Bake for 50 minutes or until the top is lightly browned. Remove the loaves from the pans immediately and cool on a rack. Cool loaves completely before storing.

Makes 2 loaves

APPLE-DATE MUFFINS

3 cups shredded apples
2 1/4 cups bran
2 tablespoons oil
1/2 cup water
2 1/4 cups oats
1 1/2 teaspoons salt
3/4 cup dates, chopped
6 tablespoons walnuts, chopped

Grind oats dry in the blender to make coarse flour. Mix all ingredients and let stand in order to wet oats and bran. Pack lightly into greased pans. Heap into muffin shapes as they do not rise. Bake in oven at 350 degrees for about 35 minutes.

Chapter One

BANANA BREAD

1 package dry yeast
¼ cup warm water
2 cups pastry flour
½ teaspoon salt
¾ cup corn syrup
⅓ cup vegetable oil
¼ cup soy milk, warmed
¼ teaspoon vanilla
3 ripe bananas, mashed
½ cup walnut pieces

Mix the yeast in warm water and set aside. Sift together the flour and salt and set aside. In a large bowl, combine the corn syrup and oil, then blend until creamy. Stir in the warm soy milk, vanilla, yeast mixture, mashed bananas, and walnut pieces. Slowly stir in the flour. Pour into a lightly oiled and floured loaf pan and let stand in a warm place for 15 minutes. Preheat the oven to 350 degrees and bake for 50 minutes.

Makes 1 loaf

BANANA BRAN MUFFINS

½ cup warm water
1 tablespoon yeast
¾ cup sugar
½ cup oil
2 cups unbleached white flour
½ teaspoon salt
3 ripe bananas
1 cup bran

Place warm water and yeast in a bowl and set aside. Mix together sugar and oil. Fold in 3 mashed bananas. Stir all into yeast mixture. Fold in 1 cup bran. Let set until bran is soft, about 10 to 15 minutes. Add flour and salt and mix well. Fill greased and floured muffin cups ¾ full. Let rise 10 minutes then bake at 350 degrees for 30 to 35 minutes.

Chapter One

CORIANDER ROLLS

1 recipe of BREAD ROLLS

FILLING

½ cup raisins
½ cup date sugar
¼ cup apple juice
2 teaspoons vegetable oil
1 teaspoon coriander
½ cup chopped walnuts

Combine the raisins, date sugar, and apple juice in a small saucepan and bring to a boil. Remove from the heat and let stand covered for 15 minutes. Follow instructions for BREAD ROLLS to the end of first rising. Cut the dough into two pieces. Roll out each piece into a rectangle ¼ inch thick and about 9 inches wide. Spread each rectangle with half of the oil, cover with half of the raisin mixture, and sprinkle with half of the coriander and chopped walnuts. Roll up tightly from the long end and seal the edges. Cut into nine slices and place, cut side down, into two oiled cake pans. Cover with a damp cloth and let rise in a warm place until doubled in bulk. Preheat the oven to 350 degrees and bake for 20 minutes or until golden brown.

Makes 18 rolls

Breads

HUSH PUPPIES

1 cup grits
3-4 cups water
1 cup onions, minced
2 tablespoons vegetable oil
1 teaspoon salt

Bring water to boil, add grits and salt. Cook for 1 hour. Cool until grits begin to get slightly stiff. Do not overcool. Add onions and oil. Spoon onto greased baking sheet. Bake at 425 degrees for about 30 to 60 minutes. Give 1 minute under broiler to brown.

OAT CRACKERS

¼ cup oil
¾ cup water
1 teaspoon salt
3 tablespoons whole wheat flour

Blend all ingredients. Add enough oats to take up water. On greased pan roll out ¼ inch thick, cut into squares, prick with fork and sprinkle lightly with salt. Bake at 250 degrees for about 1 hour.

Chapter One

OAT GEMS

1 1/3 cups water
1/2 teaspoon salt
1 tablespoon oil
1 teaspoon maple syrup
1 1/3 cups rolled oats
1/2 cup whole wheat flour

Mix all ingredients to a smooth batter, and set in a very cold place overnight. Beat a few hard strokes with a spoon, and dip while still cold into hot, oiled iron gem pans, then bake in preheated oven at 350 degrees to a nice brown.

GARLIC TOAST

6 Bread slices, (whole wheat or white)
2 tablespoons olive oil
2 cloves garlic, crushed

Mix the olive oil and crushed garlic in a small dish. Brush oil mixture onto slices of bread. Place bread under broiler until lightly browned.

Makes 6 slices

Breads

SESAME CRACKERS

½ cup water
6 tablespoons vegetable oil
½ teaspoon salt
2 cups whole wheat flour
½ cup sesame seeds

Blend water, oil, and salt in blender at medium speed until smooth. Pour into bowl and add flour and sesame seeds. Mix well and knead a little. Let rest 10 minutes. Divide into 2 parts and roll out onto oiled cookie sheet. Roll to thickness of a thin wafer. Prick with a fork and mark squares. Bake at 350 degrees for about 15 minutes.

TORTILLAS

2 cups fine corn meal
1 cup water
½ teaspoon salt

Mix and make into about 6 balls the size of a small apple. Roll each ball very thin between waxed paper. Bake slowly on burner in hot, ungreased, heavy iron skillet, turning to brown both sides.

Makes 6 tortillas

Chapter One

COCONUT CHEWS

1 2/3 cup whole wheat flour
1 1/3 cup white flour
1/4 cup wheat bran
1/3 cup coconut
1/4 cup corn syrup
1 teaspoon salt
3 tablespoons oil
3/4 cup water
1 tablespoon lecithin

Mix last six ingredients well in blender until coconut is chopped. Pour into the well-mixed dry ingredients. Roll out very thin on cookie sheets. Score and prick with a fork. Bake at 275 degrees for 45 minutes or until lightly browned.

GARLIC BREAD CHIPS

Whole Wheat Bread
Lemon Juice
Salt
Garlic and Onion Powder
Basil

Preheat the oven to 250 degrees. Using a knife, cut the bread into 1/4 inch slices. Brush each piece with a mixture made of equal parts water and lemon juice. Sprinkle with salt, garlic, onion, and basil. Bake for 1 hour or until the bread is crisp but not brown.

CROUTONS

2 teaspoons lemon juice
2 teaspoons water
3 slices whole wheat bread
salt
garlic powder

Preheat oven to 250 degrees. Mix the lemon juice and water and brush each slice of bread lightly with mixture. Place on a baking sheet, sprinkle with salt and garlic, and bake for 30 minutes. Remove from the oven, cut into 1/2 inch cubes, and return to the oven for 15 to 30 minutes or until the croutons are crisp. Do not allow croutons to darken. When completely cool, store in a plastic bag.

BREADING MEAL

1 cup fine bread crumbs, made in blender
1/2 cup yeast flakes
1/2 teaspoon salt
1 tablespoon onion salt

Dry crumbs in oven until moisture is gone. Mix ingredients. Store in a dry place up to 1 year.

Makes about 1 1/2 cups

Breakfast

BREAKFAST

Apple Icing Bread	36
Baked Apples	52
Baked Oatmeal	47
Breakfast Bars	53
Breakfast Rice Pudding	42
Buckwheat-Rice Cereal	46
Corn Meal Pancakes	40
Corn Meal Mush	45
Crunchy Granola	49
Eggless Omelet	44
French Toast	35
Fruit Juice Syrup	41
Fruit Sauce	34
Fruit Medley	52
Fruit Soup	54

Fruited Oats	46
Granola	48
Grapefruit Cup	53
Grits	45
Millet	43
Multi-Grain Waffles	36
Oat Waffles	37
Pancakes	38
Pecan Oat Waffles	37
Potato Pancakes	39
Raw Applesauce	51
Rice Fritters	42
Sauteed Breakfast Apples	51
Scrambled Tofu	54
Spiced Apple and Raisin Sauce	50
Swedish Farina	50

Chapter Two

BREAKFAST

Breakfast should be a well planned, attractively served meal which contains about one half of the day's food requirements. Plenty of time should be allowed for eating. Breakfast is the most important meal of the day. The benefit to be derived from the food depends a great deal on how long the food spends in the mouth. Thorough chewing and an unhurried attitude are essential parts of this meal. No sense of haste should be allowed. Carefully avoid using too much concentrated foods, and over enriching foods with nuts, wheat germ, seeds, or oils and sugars. Rich foods are difficult for the body to handle. It is better to use whole fruit such as grapefruit and oranges rather than their juices. The pulp is valuable nutritionally, too. If you must buy canned fruit you can get it without sugar in most markets.

DEXTRINIZING GRAINS

Dextrinization is the changing of carbohydrates from long chains as in starches to shorter chains as in dextrins. It can be done by heating starches, also by enzymatic digestion. Dextrins are nearer to being sugars, therefore taste sweeter than starch. Grains, either in whole grain berry, or as flour or grits, can be dextrinized by heating dry either in a skillet on the burner, or in a baking pan in the oven. In the first instance, stir constantly on moderately high heat for 3 to 5 minutes. In the oven allow to bake dry at 325 degrees for 5 to 10 minutes, watching carefully that it does not burn.

Breakfast

CEREAL

Cereals provide B vitamins and iron. Whole grain cereals add fiber to the diet.

Store cereal in a tightly covered container in a cool dry place.

Many grains may be used cracked or ground coarsely. Try combining two different grains such as rice and buckwheat. Use as wide a variety as is possible, but do not mix more than two or three grains in one dish. Whole kernel cereals should be cooked for several hours. General directions are: 1 cup cereal, 1 teaspoon salt, and 3-4 cups water.

When cooking cereal, add the cereal to the boiling water in a slow stream. This prevents lumping. To keep cooked cereal warm, cover the pan and remove from heat. Reheat slowly, adding water if needed.

Chapter Two

FRUIT SAUCE

Thickened fruit sauces are a healthy alternative to typical syrups for topping waffles, pancakes, and french toast, as well as for filling breakfast and dessert crepes. Any fresh or canned fruit may be thickened by following the steps below.

FOR CANNED FRUITS: Drain fruit juice into sauce pan, bring to a boil over medium heat. If more liquid than is in the can is desired, add water, or fruit juice. For each cup of liquid being thickened, mix 1 tablespoon of cornstarch in a small bowl with enough cold water to dissolve. When fruit juice is hot, add cornstarch mixture, stirring constantly until thick. Reduce heat. Cut fruit into bite size pieces and add to hot thickened juice. If desired add a little coriander, raisins, or chopped nuts. Continue cook until fruit is hot.

FOR FRESH FRUITS: Peel, core, and chop desired fruit into bite size pieces then set aside. Place desired amount of fruit juice diluted with water in sauce pan. Bring to a boil over medium heat. Reduce heat to medium and add chopped fruit. Cook until fruit reaches desired tenderness, then add 1 tablespoon of cornstarch mixed with cold water for each cup of fruit juice used, stir constantly until thick and bubbly.

FRENCH TOAST

½ cup pastry flour
1 teaspoon coriander
⅛ teaspoon salt
1 teaspoon vanilla
1 cup soy milk
1 tablespoon vegetable oil
6 slices whole wheat bread

Mix the flour, coriander and salt in a bowl. Aerate the flour with a wire whisk. In a separate small bowl, mix the soy milk, vanilla and oil, then pour into the center of the flour and mix briskly. Let the batter stand 20 minutes. Heat a lightly oiled skillet. Mix the batter well and dip each slice of bread in it to coat completely. Cook until the first side is lightly browned (about 3 minutes). Turn and cook the second side. Serve with maple syrup or FRUIT SAUCE.

Serves 2

Chapter Two

APPLE ICING BREAD

1 loaf bread dough
6 cups applesauce, slightly warm
¼ cup unsweetened coconut

Use ONE LOAF RECIPE FOR CHILDREN. Roll dough out ½" thick in large, flat baking pan, lining pan including sides. Prick dough with fork and pour on the warm applesauce. Sprinkle with the coconut. Cover with flat pan or kneading board. Let rise until dough is double in thickness. Bake 1 ¼ hours at 350 degrees. Leave in pan for one day. Heat before serving.

Serves 4-6

MULTI-GRAIN WAFFLES

½ cup rolled oats
½ cup rye flour
½ cup whole wheat flour
½ cup soy flour
2 ¼ cups water
½ teaspoon salt

Combine ingredients and blend in a blender until light and foamy. Let stand while waffle iron is heating. Batter will thicken while standing. Blend one cupful at a time just before pouring onto irons to aerate. Bake on hot waffle iron 8 to 10 minutes.

Serves 2-4

Breakfast

OAT WAFFLES

2 cups quick oats
½ cup whole wheat flour
1 teaspoon salt
⅛ cup oil
2 cups water (more may be needed depending on consistency)

Mix all ingredients and let stand for 5 minutes. Beat vigorously with a spoon adding more water if mixture is too thick, being careful not to add too much water or batter will be too thin, and waffle will be crisp and crumbly. Bake in a hot waffle iron 12 to 15 minutes or until golden brown.

Serves 2-4

PECAN OAT WAFFLES

2 cups pecan meal
1 ½ cups rolled oats
2 ¼ cups water
1 tablespoon vegetable oil
½ teaspoon salt
¼ cup chopped pecans

Combine ingredients (except chopped pecans) and blend in a blender until light and foamy. Pour ingredients into mixing bowl, and stir in nuts. Let stand while waffle iron is heating. The batter will thicken while standing. Stir briefly with spoon. Bake on hot waffle iron 8 to 10 minutes.

Serves 2-4

Chapter Two

PANCAKES

2 cups whole wheat flour
2 cups rolled oats
1 teaspoon salt
1 teaspoon coriander
4 cups soy milk
2 tablespoons oil
2 tablespoons karo syrup
1 tablespoon vanilla

Mix ingredients in a bowl. Blend 1/3 of batter at a time in blender until smooth. Place blended mixture into a bowl. Cook 1/3 cup of batter in oiled pancake griddle until edges are cooked and bottom is golden. Turn to brown other side.

Serves 4-6

POTATO PANCAKES

6 medium potatoes
1/3 cup onion, chopped fine
4 tablespoons flour
1 teaspoon salt
1/4 cup oil

Wash potatoes, leaving skins on. Leave whole or cut into large pieces. Heat 2 inches of salted water to boiling in a medium size cooking pot. Add potatoes. Cover and heat to boiling. Cook until tender; drain. Shred enough potatoes to measure 4 cups. Drain completely. Mix potatoes, onion, flour, and salt. Heat oil in a 12-inch skillet over low heat. Shape potatoes into patties. Place in skillet and cook over medium heat, turning once, until golden brown. Serve with your favorite gravy.

Serves 4-6

Chapter Two

CORN MEAL PANCAKES

1 cup whole grain flour
2 tablespoons cornstarch
1/3 cup cornmeal
1/2 teaspoon salt
1 cup water
3 tablespoons soy flour

Put flour and meal in the oven at 350 degrees for 5 minutes to lightly toast. Put all ingredients in blender and blend for 1 minute. Add more water if mixture is to thick. Place by spoonfuls onto greased pan. Bake about 15 minutes at 375 degrees until golden brown. Turn broiler on for last 1-2 minutes to brown tops (watch carefully).

Serves 2-4

FRUIT JUICE SYRUP

1 cup frozen fruit juice concentrate
1 cup water
1 1/2 tablespoons cornstarch
1 teaspoon lemon juice
1 teaspoon vanilla
1 teaspoon coriander
2 tablespoons sugar, optional

Blend all ingredients on high until well mixed. Pour into a saucepan and cook over medium heat, stirring until thick and bubbly. Serve warm over WAFFLES, PANCAKES, or FRENCH TOAST. Keep leftover syrup refrigerated.

Makes about 2 cups

Chapter Two

RICE FRITTERS

1 cup cooked RICE, salted
1/3 to 1/2 cup flour
1 tablespoon Karo
2 to 4 tablespoons water

Make a very stiff batter of the mixed ingredients. Form flat fritters. Roll in wheat germ. Bake at 350 degrees for 45 to 60 minutes or until golden brown. Serve with FRUIT SAUCE.

Serves 2

BREAKFAST RICE PUDDING

2 cups cooked RICE
1 1/2 cups NUT MILK
1/2 cups chopped walnuts
1/2 cup raisins
2 tablespoons maple syrup
1 teaspoon vanilla
1/4 teaspoon salt

Mix all ingredients and pour into oiled baking dish. Bake in oven at 350 degrees for 45 minutes.

Serves 2

Breakfast

MILLET

1 cup millet
4 cups water
1 teaspoon salt

Bring water to a boil then add millet and salt. Return to a boil. Reduce heat and cook for 45 to 60 minutes. Serve with fruit.

BAKED MILLET:

Left over millet may be placed in refrigerator and used next day sliced and baked at 350 degrees for 45 minutes. Serve baked millet with gravy.

Serves 2-4

Chapter Two

EGGLESS OMELET

1 pound firm tofu
1 cup soy milk
¼ teaspoon salt
¼ cup chopped onion
¼ cup chopped green pepper
1 teaspoon vegetable oil

Preheat oven to 400 degrees. Drain and crumble the tofu. Place the tofu, soy milk, and salt in a blender and blend until smooth. Stir in onion and green pepper. Lightly oil two 9-inch pie pans. Divide the omelet mixture between the pans, smooth out the top with a spatula, and bake for about 35 minutes. The edges will brown, the top will become golden. When the omelets are cooked cut them in half and serve, or fill with desired sauteed vegetables. May also serve topped with desired gravy.

Serves 4

Breakfast

CORN MEAL MUSH

1 cup cornmeal
1 cup water
1 teaspoon salt

Bring 2 ¾ cups water to a boil. In a bowl combine cornmeal, 1 cup water, and salt, stir until smooth. Add slowly to boiling water. Stir constantly. Bring to a boil, reduce heat, and cover. Cook over low heat 10-15 minutes, stirring occasionally. Serve hot.

Pour any remaining mush in bread pan, cover, then refrigerate. Next day, slice and bake in oven at 350 degrees for 25-30 minutes. Serve for breakfast. Top with molasses, syrup, or gravy.

GRITS

1 cup grits, stoneground, best
1 teaspoon salt
4 cups water

Bring water to a boil, add grits and salt. Reduce heat and cook gently for 1-3 hours, the longer the better. Add more grits if they are still soupy after 10 minutes of cooking, as grits should never be served runny.

Prepare a double recipe and store the extra in molds in the refrigerator. Grits congeal on cooling. Slice ½" thick, bake for 1 hour at 350 degrees. Serve with desired gravy.

Serves 4

Chapter Two

BUCKWHEAT-RICE CEREAL

½ cup buckwheat groats
1 cup brown rice
3 ½ cups water
1 teaspoon salt

Mix. Bring to boil, reduce heat and simmer covered for 2 hours.

Serves 2-4

FRUITED OATS

1 teaspoon salt
1 ¾ cups oats
⅓ cup date pieces
1 large banana, sliced

Bring 4 cups of water to a boil. Add salt, oats, and date pieces. Cook over medium heat for 15 minutes, stirring often. Remove from heat, and stir in bananas.

Serves 4

BAKED OATMEAL

1 cup chopped dates
½ cup chopped walnuts
1 ½ cups fresh fruit, chopped into bite size pieces
3 cups rolled oats
5 cups soy milk
1 teaspoon vanilla
1 teaspoon salt
1 teaspoon coriander
½ cup coconut

On the bottom of a 9" x 13" baking dish spread chopped dates and nuts. Cover with fruit. Layer oats over fruit. In a separate bowl mix vanilla, salt, coriander, and milk. Pour over oats and fruit. Sprinkle with coconut. Bake in oven at 350 degrees for 1 hour.

Serves 4-6

Chapter Two

GRANOLA

1 cup quick oats
1/2 cup whole bran cereal
1/2 cup whole wheat flour
1/2 cup flaked coconut
1/4 cup coarsely chopped slivered almonds
1/2 cup vegetable oil
1/2 cup maple syrup
1 teaspoon vanilla
1/4 cup raisins

Heat oven to 300 degrees. Mix oats, cereal, flour, coconut and almonds in ungreased oblong pan. Heat oil and syrup over medium heat until hot and bubbly; stir in vanilla. Pour syrup mixture over oat mixture; stir. Bake until light brown, 30 to 35 minutes. Stir in raisins; cool 15 minutes. Loosen granola from pan with spatula; cool to room temperature. Break granola into pieces. Cover and store no longer than 1 week.

Breakfast

CRUNCHY GRANOLA

2 ½ cups rolled oats
1 cup shredded coconut
¾ cup coarsely chopped almonds
½ cup sunflower seeds
½ cup corn syrup
¼ cup vegetable oil
½ cup chopped dried pineapple
½ cup raisins

In a bowl stir together oats, coconut, almonds, and sunflower seeds. Combine corn syrup and oil; stir into oat mixture. Spread out evenly on a cookie sheet. Bake at 300 degrees for 45-50 minutes or until light brown, stirring every 10-15 minutes. Remove from oven; stir in pineapple and raisins. Transfer into another pan for cooling, stirring often to prevent lumping. Store in tightly covered jars or plastic bags. Do not store for more than 2 weeks.

Chapter Two

SPICED APPLE AND RAISIN SAUCE

1 cup coarsely chopped red apple
1 1/2 teaspoons oil
1/4 cup raisins
1/2 teaspoon coriander
2 tablespoons cornstarch
1 1/2 cups water
2 tablespoons lemon juice

In medium skillet, cook apple in oil until tender. Stir in raisins and coriander. In small bowl, combine remaining ingredients; blend well. Stir into apple mixture; cook until thick, stirring constantly. Serve warm. Makes approximately 2 cups of sauce. May use as a cereal topping.

SWEDISH FARINA

2/3 cups rye flour
2 3/4 cups water
1 teaspoon salt
1/2 cup raisins

Whip the rye flour into the water. Add salt. Do not have lumps in mixture. Stir rapidly while cooking over high heat. When it begins to boil turn heat to low, add raisins, and cook for 10 minutes, stirring occasionally. The mush thickens while cooling.

Serves 2

Breakfast

SAUTEED BREAKFAST APPLES

4 cups shredded apples with peelings
1 tablespoon lemon juice
2 tablespoons vegetable oil
Salt to taste

Heat oil in a fry pan, add shredded apples and lemon juice. Stir constantly for 4 minutes. Reduce heat, cover and continue cooking for 10 minutes. Serve over oatmeal or CRUNCHY GRANOLA.

Serves 4-6

RAW APPLESAUCE

4 medium eating apples, cut up
1/4 cup light corn syrup
2 tablespoons lemon juice
Dash of salt

Place half of the apples and the remaining ingredients in blender and blend until smooth. Add remaining apples; repeat.

Makes about 2 cups

Chapter Two

BAKED APPLES

Core baking apples (Rome Beauty, Golden Delicious). Place apples upright in ungreased baking dish. Place 1 to 2 tablespoons maple syrup or light corn syrup, 1/8 teaspoon coriander, and 2 tablespoons GRANOLA in center of each apple. Pour water (1/4 inch deep) into baking dish. Bake uncovered in oven at 375 degrees until tender when pierced with fork, 30 to 40 minutes. Spoon syrup in dish over apples several times during baking if desired.

FRUIT MEDLEY

1 cup seedless green grapes
1 cup cantaloupe balls
1 cup pineapple cubes
1 cup strawberries
1 can (6 ounces) frozen orange juice concentrate, partially thawed

Divide fruit among 6 dessert dishes. Just before serving, spoon 1 to 2 tablespoons orange juice concentrate onto each serving, and sprinkle with chopped nuts or coconut.

BREAKFAST BARS

1 cup shredded raw apple
1 1/2 cups rolled oats
2 tablespoons vegetable oil
3/4 cup water
1/2 teaspoon salt
1/2 cup chopped dates
1/2 cup chopped almonds
1 teaspoon coriander
1 teaspoon vanilla

Blend oats in blender on high to make oat flour. Pour into bowl and mix with remaining ingredients. Press into oiled baking dish. Bake in oven at 375 degrees for 25 minutes. Cut into bars when cool.

Serves 4

GRAPEFRUIT CUP

2 grapefruit
1 pint strawberries
1/4 cup maple syrup

Cut grapefruit into halves. Cut around edges and membranes to remove grapefruit sections. Place sections in bowl. Remove membranes from grapefruit shells and reserve shells. Cut strawberries into halves and place in bowl with grapefruit sections. Pour maple syrup over fruit; toss. Cover and refrigerate. Just before serving, fill grapefruit shells with fruit mixture. Garnish with flaked coconut if desired.

Chapter Two

FRUIT SOUP

3 tablespoons maple syrup
3 tablespoons cornstarch
1/8 teaspoon salt
1 1/4 cup white grape juice
1 cup water
1 cup cranberry juice
3 cups assorted fresh fruit

Mix cornstarch with small amount of white grape juice. Place remaining grape juice and water in saucepan with cornstarch mixture and salt. Heat to boiling, stirring constantly. Boil and stir 1 minute. Remove from heat; stir in cranberry juice. Cover loosely and refrigerate until chilled. Stir in fruit. Serve over GRANOLA.

SCRAMBLED TOFU

2 tablespoons vegetable oil
1/4 teaspoon garlic powder
1/4 cup minced, sauteed onions
1/2 teaspoon salt
2 cups cubed tofu

Heat all ingredients in a skillet. Mix well with fork. For variation add 2 tablespoons minced, sauteed green pepper.

Serves 2

Breakfast

Notes

Nondairy Milks

NONDAIRY MILKS

Almond Milk	68
Cashew Milk	67
Coconut Milk	63
Fresh Apple Milk	64
Madison Milk	64
Maple Walnut Milk	69
Raw Nut Milk	63
Soy Milk	65
Strawberry Date Milk	67
Walnut Milk	66

Notes

Chapter Three

DAIRY PRODUCT SUBSTITUTES

It is widely held that milk is essential for all, adults and children. The human being is the only animal that takes milk into adult life. All other animals can get sufficient nutrients from solid food. What is the condition of man? Must he have milk?

While cow's milk may be the perfect food for a baby cow, it is far from perfect for the baby human and may be even worse for the adult. The balance of the major nutrients is improper for a baby, and the content of amino acids in the proteins is improper for the neurologic development of the child; causing the brain and nerve development to be less than ideal. A baby calf does not need a very highly developed brain, but the baby human has tremendous development of brain tissue during the first year of life, when his mother's milk would stimulate just such growth, because of very different cystine/methionine ratios in human milk as compared to cow's milk.. Certain amino acids are much too high in cow's milk, and may actually be toxic to human infants. The chemistry of milk is as species specific as is the fingerprint. When the baby human is weaned from the breast, he should be weaned to the table, not to formula. There are several diseases that either do not occur in the breast-fed infant, or occur with much less frequency than in bottle-fed infants, including infantile eczema, obesity, colic, allergies, and sudden infant death syndrome (crib deaths). If even the mother drinks milk, her breast milk may cause the baby to have allergies or colic. (1)

There are also problems for the adult who drinks milk, starting with sensitivity. A milk sensitivity is the commonest food sensitivity in America today. It often masquerades as an apparently unrelated disorder, making a recognition of the true source of the problem difficult. Minerals in milk are imbalanced for the adult: (1) Calcium is too abundant in milk, and tends to cause adults to form stones and to deposit calcium plaques in their blood vessels. Nutritionists agree that the minimum daily requirement of calcium has been set far too high for adults. There is good evidence that many Americans get too much calcium. Milk is high in sodium, as breasts are simply modified sweat glands which put out much salt. Blood pressure and kidney problems may result from taking too much sodium. The

Nondairy Milks

sweatglands, kidneys, and possibly other glands are damaged from too much sodium.

Milk is low in iron, yet, adult women need a generous quantity of iron from their diet. Milk displaces other food from the diet that could yield good quantities of iron. The minerals in milk were not designed for adults.

Milk increases cholesterol and other blood fats. Milk is probably more likely than any other food to raise the blood cholesterol. There is an increased likelihood of getting infectious diseases of several kinds if one uses milk. Milk-borne infections include many fevers that make one think that he has influenza or a cold, but it is actually a milk-borne virus or Salmonella. One large outbreak of Salmonella dysentery; was from nonfat dry skim milk. There are many other diseases that are transmitted by milk. One of the most troublesome microorganisms in milk is that of cancer virus particles. Cancer viruses are excreted into the milk from the bloodstream of the affected animal.

Lactose is milk sugar; casein is milk protein. In infancy, there are two special enzymes produced in the infant stomach to digest these two nutrients. Without these special enzymes, lactase for the digestion of lactose and rennin for the digestion of casein, milk is not easy to digest. At about 18 to 24 months, rennin forever ceases being produced; and lactase diminishes markedly or disappears entirely in large racial groups comprising up to 70% of the world's population. This seems to be nature's way of saying that this is the terminal point for the need of milk. Since milk has no fiber, and tends to form hard, difficult-to-move feces, constipation is more likely to occur in those who drink milk.

In summary, we can say that cow's milk is far from the perfect food, even for babies. Everybody does not need milk, and babies need the special milk that was designed for their own species. When one has been weaned, he has outgrown his need for milk.

(1) Medical Tribune, Dec. 6, 1978. page 3

Chapter Three

CALCIUM

Everybody needs some calcium. There are a variety of vegetarian foods rich in this mineral.

Food Source	Quantity	Calcium mg
Soy milk		
Soyagen, all purpose	1 cup	72 mg
Soyameal, all purpose	1 cup	150 mg
Broccoli, cooked	1 cup	117 mg
Collards, cooked	1 cup	304 mg
Mustard greens, cooked	1 cup	278 mg
Sesame seed, whole	2 T	258 mg
Sunflower seed kernels	2 T	27 mg
Soy beans, cooked	1 cup	146 mg
Kale, cooked	1 cup	224 mg
Oatmeal cereal, cooked	1 cup	191 mg
Cream of wheat, cooked	1 cup	185 mg

Nondairy Milks

RAW NUT MILK

1 cup raw nuts (almonds should be blanched)
3 ½ cups water
1 tablespoon maple syrup
Dash of salt

Blend all ingredients in a blender for 5 minutes. Strain through a sieve and press all of the liquid out of the pulp. Chill.

Makes about 1 quart

COCONUT MILK

1 cup fresh coconut
3 cups water, including coconut liquid
1 teaspoon karo
dash of salt

Blend all ingredients in blender until smooth. May be strained or used on cereal unstrained. Dried coconut may be used if fresh coconut is unavailable.

Makes about 3 cups

Chapter Three

MADISON MILK

1 ½ pounds dry soybeans
3 teaspoons salt
1 cup vegetable oil
1 ¾ cup Karo

Soak the soybeans overnight, drain and grind fine in the blender with sufficient water to make 1 gallon total mixture. Heat in a large kettle, stirring continuously until finger cannot be held in mixture because of heat. Strain through a cheesecloth or muslin, squeezing out the milk. Boil for 45 minutes, stirring constantly. Take 2 cups of the hot milk and blend for 5 minutes in blender along with the oil, salt, and Karo. Return to kettle. Boil 15 minutes. Add water to make 5 quarts. Refrigerate.

Makes about 5 quarts

FRESH APPLE MILK

Place 2 cups RAW NUT MILK in blender. Add 4 washed apples which have been chopped into 1 inch chunks. (Remove stems, seeds, cores, and peels.) Blend 1 to 2 minutes.

Makes about 4 cups

Nondairy Milks

SOY MILK

1 cup dry soybeans
1 cup coconut
2 tablespoons corn syrup
2 teaspoons vanilla
1/4 teaspoon salt

Soak beans overnight in 4 cups water. Rinse and drain beans. Place soybeans into saucepan with 5 cups water and coconut. Cover and bring to a boil. Reduce heat and simmer for 25 minutes. Remove from heat. Place 1 cup of cooked beans and coconut into a blender with 1 cup water, and blend until creamy. Add 3 more cups of water to blender, and blend 1 more minute. Strain several times through a cheesecloth. Pour into a pitcher. Repeat procedure with another cup of beans until all beans are blended. Chill.

Chapter Three

WALNUT MILK

1 cup water
1 cup walnuts
2 tablespoons maple syrup
¼ teaspoon salt
1 teaspoon vanilla
3 cups water

Blend all but last ingredient on high until creamy. Stop blender and add remaining water. Blend. Pour into pitcher and serve. Refrigerate left over milk in covered container.

Makes about 4 cups

STRAWBERRY DATE MILK

1 ¼ cups water
1 cup cashew pieces
6 pitted dates
1 teaspoon vanilla
1 cup frozen white grape juice concentrate
¼ teaspoon salt
4 cups strawberries

Blend all but last ingredient on high until creamy. Stop blender and add strawberries. Blend briefly. Pour into pitcher and serve. Refrigerate left over milk in covered container.

Makes about 4 cups

CASHEW MILK

1 cup cashew pieces
4 cups water
¼ cup corn syrup
2 teaspoons vanilla
¼ teaspoon salt

Blend cashews and 1 cup of the water on high until creamy. Stop the blender and add remaining ingredients. Blend briefly to mix. Place in a pitcher and serve. Refrigerate left over milk in covered container.

Makes about 4 cups

Chapter Three

ALMOND MILK

1 ½ cups water
1 cup blanched almonds
2 tablespoons corn syrup
½ teaspoon vanilla
¼ teaspoon almond flavoring
¼ teaspoon coriander
¼ teaspoon salt
2 cups water

Blend all but last ingredient on high until creamy. Stop blender and add remaining water. Blend briefly to mix. Pour into pitcher and serve. Refrigerate left over milk in covered container.

Makes about 4 cups

Nondairy Milks

MAPLE WALNUT MILK

1 1/2 cups water
3/4 cups walnuts
15 pitted dates
1 1/2 teaspoons maple flavoring
3/4 teaspoon vanilla
1/2 teaspoon coriander
1/4 teaspoon salt
2 1/2 cups water

Blend all but last ingredient on high until creamy. Stop blender and add remaining water. Blend briefly to mix. Pour into pitcher and serve. Refrigerate left over milk in covered container.

Makes about 4 cups

Entrees

ENTREES

Baked Beans	123
Baked Macaroni	144
Baked Vegi-Burgers	114
Beans and Greens	129
Beans and Pasta	124
Black Beans	128
Black-Eyed Pea Potpourri	125
Burritos	95
Cabbage Casserole	145
Carrot Rice Loaf	143
Cashew Garbanzo Bake	120
Cashew Rice Roast	140
Chili	126
Chili-n-Grits	104
Chinese Pepper Steak	136
Corn Tamale Pie	96
Country Bread Stuffing	106
Creole	121
Crepes	98

East India Black-Eyed Peas	122
Fancy Mashed Potato Bake	89
Fri Chic and Pasta	149
Fried Rice	141
Garbanzo Pot Pie	121
Garbanzos and Pasta	147
Goulash	146
Great Northern Stew	112
Green Beans and Potato Casserole	90
Haystacks	97
Hearty Hash	88
Hoppin' John	141
Irish Stew	110
Italian Lentils	133
Italian Potato Dumplings	105
Jambalaya	139
Lasagna	152
Lentil Casserole	135
Lentil-Nut Roast	131

Lentils and Noodles	134
Lima Bean and Tomato Casserole	126
Lima Broccoli Bake	130
Macaroni and Chee	144
Mexican Garbanzos	122
Oat Burgers or Loaf	118
Oat Crepes	99
Pasta Primavera	150
Pecan Herb Loaf	86
Peppers and Pasta	148
Pizza	102
Potato Pie	87
Refried Beans	127
Rice Medley	143
Savory Millet Patties	117
Shepherd Pie	101
Spanish Rice	142
Split Pea Patties	116
Split Peas and Rice Casserole	131
Stuffed Cabbage Rolls	107

Stuffed Manicotti	151
Stuffed Peppers	90
Sukiyaki	137
Summer Squash and Beans	93
Sun Patties	119
Sunflower "Beefy" Pot Pie	108
Sweet and Sour Lentils	132
Tofu Burgers	115
Tofu Meat Balls	100
Tostadas	101
Vegetable Chow Mein	138
Vegetable Lasagna	153
Vegetable Stew	111
Vegetable Stuffed Baked Potatoes	91
Vegetarian Meat Loaf	100
Vegetarian Steaks	113
Walnut Balls	103
Zucchini Boats	94
Zucchini Casserole	92

Chapter four

BASIC COOKING DIRECTIONS FOR LEGUMES AND RICE

BEANS •

Black:
Black-eyed peas:
Great Northern:
Kidney:
Lima:
Navy:
Pinto: Sort beans and rinse. Cover with 2" cold water. Soak overnight, or bring to a boil for 2 minutes, remove from heat, cover and let stand for 1 hour. Cook over medium heat until tender (about 2 hours). Add salt during last 30 minutes of cooking.

Garbanzos: Sort peas and rinse. Cover with 2" cold water. Soak overnight. Bring to a boil, reduce heat to medium, cover, cook 6-8 hours. Add salt during last 30 minutes of cooking.

Lentils: Sort and rinse. Cover with 1" cold water. Soak for 1 hour. Bring to a boil, reduce heat to medium and cook for 30 minutes. Add salt. Continue cooking for 20-30 minutes, or until tender.

Entrees

Split Peas: Rinse peas. Cover with 2" cold water. Bring to a boil, reduce heat to medium, cover and simmer 1-2 hours. Add salt during last 30 minutes of cooking. Stir occasionally to prevent burning. For thicker soup, remove cover after peas are soft and continue to cook over low heat, stirring often until desired thickness.

RICE •

Brown: Bring 2 1/2 cups water and 1 teaspoon salt to a boil. Add 1 cup brown rice. Reduce heat to low, cover, and simmer 40-50 minutes or until water is soaked up.

White: Bring 2 1/2 cups water and 1 teaspoon salt to a boil. Add 1 cup white rice. Reduce heat to low, cover, and simmer for 30 minutes or until water is soaked up.

Chapter four

RICE ADDITIONS:

Confetti Rice: Stir 1 cup cooked frozen mixed vegetables and ½ teaspoon dried dillweed into hot cooked RICE.

Herbed Rice: Add 1 teaspoon dried thyme and ½ teaspoon basil to RICE while cooking.

Nutty Rice: Add ½ cup slivered almonds and ¼ cup sliced green onions, and ½ teaspoon coriander to hot cooked RICE.

Parsley Rice: Stir ¼ cup snipped parsley into hot cooked RICE.

NUTS

Nuts are concentrated foods and should be used in small quantities. No more than 1/6 to 1/10 of any dish should be of nuts. They should never be eaten between meals. Frying nuts or roasting in oil makes them harder to digest. If eaten fresh or slightly roasted, they are easily digested. Commercially obtained raw nuts should be sterilized in the oven at 300 degrees for 15 minutes. This practice is especially important for nuts obtained from foreign countries.

Entrees

PASTA

Most people think pasta is no more than macaroni and cheese, or spaghetti. A vast array of main dishes can be made with pastas. Combine spaghetti with steamed or sauteed vegetables, or just plain olive oil, fresh garlic, and plenty of freshly chopped onions. Use your ingenuity to create your own dishes.

The use of whole grain pastas by Italians is credited with giving them a very low incidence of both heart trouble and cancer. The fiber of whole grains is very effective in keeping the cholesterol low and in maintaining good bowel health, free from ulcers, diverticula, polyps, and cancer.

Pasta should be cooked to the point where it is still a bit firm, but no longer starchy. To test pasta for doneness taste it. When done, drain immediately to prevent further cooking.

To keep pasta hot for a short time, return drained to empty cooking pan, add a little olive oil and cover with a lid. To keep pasta hot for longer periods of time, place the colander of pasta over a pan containing a small amount of boiling water. Coat pasta with a little olive oil to keep from sticking, and cover colander.

Reduce the cooking time by $1/3$ for pasta that will be cooked again in a casserole.

Cook very thin pasta for 5 to 6 minutes. Cook medium-thin pasta for 9 to 12 minutes. Cook medium-thick pasta for about 15 minutes. Cook very thick pastas for 15-25 minutes.

Immediately after cooking drain pasta in colander, do not rinse.

Chapter four

RICE

The world produces more rice than any other grain. Because it was found that rice keeps better for shipping and storage when polished, white rice has largely replaced brown or natural rice. This is a great pity because white rice has been robbed of much of its nutrient value and flavor.

Rice is highly nutritious and easily digested, being almost completely assimilated. It is the least allergenic of all foods. When it is milled so that only the husks are removed, the product is whole, brown, or natural rice. Brown rice contains about 8% protein of very good biologic value, little fat, and 79% carbohydrate (chiefly starch). It has a good supply of minerals, including calcium, phosphorus, iron, and copper traces. The vitamins include B1, B2, niacin, and E. There are many essential micronutrients.

Brown rice retains more fiber and nutrients than milled rice because less of the bran is removed. It must cook longer and remains chewy when done. Slender, dark grains of wild rice have a nutty flavor and require longer cooking time also. Regular milled rice has its husk removed and the grain is cleaned and polished. Parboiled rice keeps more of its nutrients because it is steamed under pressure before milling.

Test rice for doneness by pinching a grain between your thumb and forefinger. If there is no hard core, the rice is done.

Cooked rice may be frozen or refrigerated. To reheat, add 2 tablespoons of water for each cup of cooked rice. Cover and simmer until hot.

SEASONING GUIDE

Spices and herbs include a variety of vegetable products which are aromatic and have pungent flavors. They are used to enhance the natural flavors of foods. Many herbs add certain of the trace elements to the daily dietary. Many of these trace elements are difficult to obtain from any other source.

Herbs are from the leafy parts of the temperate zone plants. Certain non-toxic seeds may also be used to flavor foods. Care to avoid any irritating herb will be richly repaid in good health of the stomach. Herbs gradually lose flavor and color during storage. They should not be purchased in large quantity. Store them in a cool, dry place in airtight containers to retard loss of flavor.

Spices are defined as parts of plants, such as the seeds, buds, fruit, flowers, bark or roots of plants, usually of tropical origin. They are sold whole or ground. Several spices are irritating to the stomach and to the nerves. These irritating spices should be avoided.

Chapter four

Below is a list of safe seasonings and their common uses in cooking. These seasonings may be added or substituted for any that are used in recipes in this book. Feel free to experiment. Start with 1/4 teaspoon for each 4 servings; then taste before adding more. When substituting fresh herbs for dried herbs, use three times more fresh than dried.

BASIL is used in stews, stuffing, vegetables, pasta, salads, dips, and sauces.

BAY LEAF is used in dried bean dishes, rice, and gravies.

CELERY salt or seeds are used in sauces, stews, stuffings, and spreads.

CLOVES are used in cookies, fruit salads, and vegetables.

CORIANDER is used in bean dishes, fruit salads, cookies, and pastries.

CUMIN is used in Mexican dishes, dips, and spreads.

DILL weed or seed is used in vegetables, dressings, breads, and sauces.

FENNEL is used in vegetables and sauces.

GARLIC is used in stews, stuffing, vegetables, pasta, casseroles, gravies and sauces.

LEMON OR ORANGE PEEL is used in spreads, relishes, fruit soup, fruit salads, breads, desserts, and sauces.

MARJORAM is used in stews, casseroles, vegetables, gravies, and sauces.

Entrees

MINT is used in vegetables, salads, stewed fruits, and sauces.

ONION is used in stews, stuffing, vegetables, pasta, casseroles, gravies, sauces, dips, and spreads.

OREGANO is used in stews, casseroles, vegetables, and salads.

PAPRIKA is used mainly as a garnish.

PARSLEY is used in casseroles, vegetables, gravies, sauces, and as a garnish.

ROSEMARY is used in stews, casseroles, vegetables, and salads.

SAGE is used in stews, stuffing, vegetables, gravies, and sauces.

SAVORY is used in stews, casseroles, stuffing, vegetables, gravies and sauces.

THYME is used in "meat" loaves, stews, casseroles, vegetables, sauces, and spreads.

IRRITATING SEASONINGS

Black Pepper	Mustard Seed
Chilipeppers	Ginger
Cayenne	Nutmeg
Horseradish	Vinegar
Cloves	Baking soda, powder
Cinnamon	Hungarian Paprika

Chapter four

PROTEINS AND B-VITAMINS

Entrees should supply either a good quality or a good quantity of protein, and generous amounts of B-vitamins. The body requires a steady supply of proteins for growth and repair, and the mind must have readily available B-vitamins for proper thinking and steady nerves. Vegetables and fruits, grains and nuts supply all the food elements needed by a healthy person to maintain health. If one is concerned about vitamin B-12 intake, he may easily supplement his diet with certain food yeasts which have been produced in such a way as to contain this vitamin, or with commercially available B-12. One can thus maintain the advantages of avoiding animal products and still get sufficient B-12 to meet the National Research Council recommendation.

Nuts, seeds, legumes, and grains all make suitable entrees. Many root vegetables when mixed with nuts make good entrees. The greens have such a good quality of protein that their presence in a meal in generous amounts makes the protein content of other foods of less importance.

Entrees

FATS

Most people agree that the addition of fat improves the flavor of food. However, there is a point at which adding more fat will not continue to improve the flavor, but will simply make it feel more greasy and add more calories. Usually a small fraction of the fat customarily added will be quite adequate to achieve the desired flavor enhancement. To add more fat simply produces a larger problem for the body to handle.

Fats circulate through the blood, liver, eyes, blood vessels, kidneys, and other tissues to bring an increased risk of disease in each organ that they spend much time in. Fats are concentrated foods and cannot be handled in the blood very easily in the biochemical systems of the body. Generally speaking, we may eat freely of fruits, vegetables, and whole grains, but must eat sparingly of all other foods.

Fat is a less compressible liquid than water. As the heart squeezes down on the blood which has little fat in it, it is easily compressible and squeezed into the major arteries. As the level of fat increases, the blood becomes less compressible, increasing the likelihood of heart disease.

There are many benefits of a low fat diet. One of the most important is a reduction in coronary heart disease.

Many recipes in this cook book call for sauteed onions, garlic, or celery. If you are trying to follow a low fat diet, or an oil free diet, simply replace the oil with water. You will most likely need more water than the amount of oil called for.

If you do choose to use oil as the recipes call for, use Safflower, Corn, or Olive oil, as these are the best.

Chapter four

PECAN HERB LOAF

½ onion, finely chopped
1 teaspoon olive oil
2 large garlic cloves, finely chopped
¾ cup chopped pecans
½ cup chopped almonds
2 tablespoons soy flour
2 tablespoon cornstarch powder
4 tablespoon nutritional yeast
1 ½ teaspoons salt
½ teaspoon basil
¼ teaspoon oregano
¼ teaspoon savory
¾ teaspoon garlic powder
20 ounces firm tofu
5 tablespoons raw tahini

Saute the onion in olive oil over medium heat for 3 minutes. Add the garlic and cook for 2 more minutes. Place the pecans and almonds in a food processor or blender. Chop until the nuts have the texture of very coarse corn meal. Combine the nuts, soy flour, cornstarch, yeast, salt, basil, oregano, savory, and garlic powder in a large mixing bowl and mix well. Place the tofu, half at a time, in a clean dish cloth (do not use cheesecloth). Collect the corners and wring tightly to expel as much water as possible. The tofu will crumble. Break up any large pieces. Combine the tofu thoroughly with the onion mixture and tahini. Add to the dry ingredients and combine well. Press firmly into an oiled loaf pan and bake at 350 degrees for 1 hour. Serve with desired gravy. Use leftovers for sandwiches.

THIS RECIPE CAN ALSO BE USED FOR BURGERS. Just press mixture firmly into patties and bake at 350 degrees in an oiled baking dish for 35 minutes or until firm and brown.

Serves 6

POTATO PIE

Unbaked 9-inch classic double crust. Add ¼ teaspoon each garlic and onion salt to the flour.

FILLING

3 tablespoons oil
1 large onion, diced
2 carrots, diced and cooked
3 medium-size potatoes, cubed and cooked
1 cup green peas, cooked if frozen
2 green onion tops, chopped
2 cups soy milk
3 tablespoons cornstarch
½ teaspoon salt

Heat oven to 425 degrees. For filling, heat oil in small saucepan. Add onion and cook until tender. Add carrots. Saute two minutes. Place potatoes and peas in large bowl. Add sauteed mixture and onion tops. Mix cornstarch with small amount of the soy milk then add to remaining soy milk; mix well. Add to potato mixture along with salt. Spoon into unbaked pie shell. Moisten pastry edge with water. Cover with top crust. Fold top edge under bottom crust. Flute with fork. Cut slits in top crust for steam to escape. Bake for 20 to 25 minutes or until crust is golden brown. Serve warm.

Serves 4-6

Chapter four

HEARTY HASH

2 cups cooked RICE
½ cup onions, sauteed
½ cup chopped celery, sauteed
¼ cup brewers yeast flakes
2 tablespoons vegetable oil
½ teaspoon salt
¼ teaspoon garlic powder
2 tablespoon soy sauce
2 cups shredded raw potatoes

Mix all ingredients well. Spoon into hot skillet. Cover and cook for 10 minutes. Turn, stir, cover and cook for 10 to 15 minutes longer.

Serves 4

Entrees

FANCY MASHED POTATO BAKE

10 medium potatoes, peeled and cut up to boil for mashing
6 carrots, peeled, sliced and cooked until tender
2 cups garbanzos, cooked and drained
3 stalks celery, sliced thin
1 medium onion, chopped
1 cup cooked frozen peas, or canned peas
3 tablespoons oil
1 1/2 recipes CASHEW GRAVY

Cook and mash potatoes. Saute onions and celery in oil. Spread 1/2 of the mashed potatoes on the bottom of oiled, long baking dish. Layer carrots, garbanzos, peas, celery, and onions on top of mashed potatoes. Pour gravy evenly over vegetables. With remaining mashed potatoes make 12 mashed potato balls, form with hands. Place balls evenly on top of gravy and vegetables. Sprinkle lightly with paprika and parsley flakes for decoration. Bake at 400 degrees for 20 minutes.

Serves 6

Chapter four

GREEN BEANS AND POTATO CASSEROLE

1 1/2 cups cooked fresh green beans, or canned green beans
1 cup potatoes, diced and cooked
1/2 cup celery, diced
1/4 cup imitation bacon bits
1 medium onion, chopped
2 cups soy milk
1/3 cup bread crumbs

Combine beans, potatoes, and bacon bits. Place in oiled 1 quart casserole dish. Saute onion and celery in 2 tablespoons vegetable oil until tender. Add flour and stir to a smooth paste. Add milk. Cook, stirring constantly until thickened. Pour over vegetables in casserole dish and stir well. Sprinkle with bread crumbs. Bake in oven at 350 degrees for 30 minutes.

Serves 4

STUFFED PEPPERS

Wash 6 Bell Peppers. Cut in half lengthwise or if not too big slice off the top and fill one for each person. Stuff with SPANISH RICE. Sprinkle with paprika. Bake at 375 degrees for 1 hour.

Serves 6

VEGETABLE STUFFED BAKED POTATOES

6 large baking potatoes
1 large onion, chopped and sauteed
1 cup canned or fresh green peas
1 cup carrots, peeled, diced and boiled until tender, then drained
½ cup soy milk

Bake potatoes in oven at 375 degrees until tender all the way through. Remove from oven. Cut a slice off the top of each potato and gently scoop out potato from shell being careful not to tear shell. Place potato filling in bowl, and mix with soy milk until smooth and creamy. Season with salt and onion powder. In the bottom of each empty potato shell spoon equal amounts of each: onion, peas, and carrots. Finish filling each potato shell with mashed potato mixture. Sprinkle each with paprika and parsley flakes if desired. Place filled potato shells on a cookie sheet and bake in oven at 350 degrees for 20 minutes or until hot.

Serves 6

Chapter four

ZUCCHINI CASSEROLE

2 pounds zucchini, sliced and cooked
2 cups potatoes, cubed, cooked and drained
Salt to taste
3 tablespoons oil
1/2 cup onion, minced
1 1/2 cups soy milk
4 tablespoons flour
1 cup soft bread crumbs

In oiled casserole dish arrange layers of zucchini and potatoes. Saute onion in oil until tender. Place flour and 1/2 cup of the soy milk in a plastic container and cover with a lid. Shake vigorously until smooth. Add flour mixture and remaining soy milk to onions, cook over medium heat until thick. Add desired seasonings and continue to cook over low heat for 5 minutes stirring constantly to prevent scorching. Pour sauce over layered ingredients in casserole dish. Top with crumbs. Bake at 350 degrees for 1 hour.

Serves 6

Entrees

SUMMER SQUASH AND BEANS

1 cup dried navy beans
1 large onion, chopped
1 tablespoon oil
2 yellow squash, sliced
2 medium zucchini squash, sliced
2 tablespoons vegetable oil
2 cups bean sprouts
Salt to taste

Cook beans according to basic directions on package until tender. Drain. Saute onion in oil until lightly browned. Combine with drained beans and remove from heat. In a large skillet, fry and stir squash in vegetable oil until tender-crisp. Add sprouts and fry another minute. Add salt to beans and squash. In a large shallow oiled casserole dish, spread half of the bean mixture evenly on bottom. Then layer squash evenly over beans. Make a third layer with remaining beans. Cover with seasoned bread crumbs and bake in oven at 350 degrees for 30 minutes.

Serves 4-6

Chapter four

ZUCCHINI BOATS

3/4 cup dried navy beans
6 medium zucchini squash
1 large onion, chopped
1 clove garlic, crushed
2 tablespoons olive oil
1 16-ounce can tomato sauce
Salt
1 teaspoon Italian seasoning
4 cups fresh whole wheat bread cubes
1/4 cup chopped parsley

Cook beans according to basic directions. Drain. Parboil whole zucchini for 8 minutes. Drain and cool. Saute onion and garlic in olive oil until onion is transparent. Add tomato sauce, salt, and Italian seasoning. Simmer for 15 minutes. Cut a slice, about 1/4 inch deep, along the side of each squash. Hollow it out, leaving about 1/4 inch shell for the boats. Chop the zucchini trimmings and add to the sauce. Cook sauce until zucchini is tender. Add a little water if sauce becomes too thick. Remove 3/4 cups of the sauce, reserve and keep hot. Stir bread cubes, beans, and parsley into remaining sauce. Fill zucchini boats with this stuffing and place in oiled baking dish. Bake in a preheated 350 degree oven 40 minutes. Spoon some of the reserved sauce over zucchini boats.

Serves 6

BURRITOS

1 medium onion, cut into thin wedges
1 green pepper, membranes and seeds removed, cut into thin strips
1 teaspoon olive oil
1 1/2 cups PINTO BEANS, cooked and mashed
1 cup cooked RICE
1 cup canned tomatoes, chopped
6 tortillas, warmed
1 cup SALSA
1 cup sliced black olives

Saute the green pepper and onion in the olive oil over medium heat until tender. In a saucepan, mix the rice and tomatoes and heat. On each warm tortilla place equal amounts of mashed pinto beans, rice, green pepper, and black olives. Cover with salsa and roll up, folding over the ends. Serve topped with GUACAMOLE if desired.

Makes 6 burritos

Chapter four

CORN TAMALE PIE

1 cup corn meal
2 ½ cups water
2 cups whole kernel corn
¾ cup black olives, sliced
1 cup onion, chopped
½ cup tomato sauce
1 teaspoon salt

Make CORN MEAL MUSH of corn meal, water, and salt. Simmer remaining ingredients until onion is beginning to be transparent. Place half of the mush in a baking dish. Pour corn-onion mixture on top of mush. Make a third layer with remainder of mush. Bake at 350 degrees for 1 hour.

Serves 4

Entrees

HAYSTACKS

Corn chips
PINTO BEANS (cooked and seasoned)
Lettuce, shredded
Avacado, peeled, pitted, and diced
Tomatoes, diced
Onions, finely chopped
Black Olives, sliced
CHEE SAUCE (optional)
SOUR CREAM (optional)

This meal is particularly enjoyable in the summer time when it is too hot to cook for hours over the stove. The way to prepare this dish is simply to layer the ingredients onto your dinner plate as follows:

Layer of corn chips, put hot beans over chips, then lettuce, tomatoes, onions, and olives. For those who like sauces the CHEE SAUCE is nice, or SOUR CREAM. For those who do not wish to use a prepared sauce, but would like the added moisture just use the broth from the cooked pinto beans.

Chapter four

CREPES

¾ cup whole wheat pastry flour
¼ teaspoon salt
2 teaspoons vegetable oil
1 ¼ cups soy milk

Sift together the flour and salt. Combine 2 tablespoons of oil and soy milk and mix well. Pour the soy milk mixture into the flour and mix well. If there are lumps, beat with an eggbeater for 30 seconds. Heat an 8-inch, nonstick, coated skillet, or coat an uncoated skillet with a thin film of lecithin. When a drop of water sizzles on the skillet, the skillet is ready to cook the crepes. Pour a couple of tablespoons of the batter into the skillet, immediately tipping the skillet around in all directions to coat the bottom completely. Cook until the crepe is golden brown, about 1 minute. Loosen the edges of the crepe from the skillet and turn over with a spatula. Cook for another minute. Repeat until all the batter is used up.

Crepes can be used as a breakfast dish, a dinner entree, or a dessert, depending on what filling is used.

BREAKFAST SUGGESTIONS: Any kind of fresh or canned fruit chopped into small pieces. For variety, mix crushed granola to fruit filling.

DINNER SUGGESTIONS: Any kind of cooked or steamed vegetable. Sauteed onions mixed with cooked vegetables is a delightful combination. Serve topped with desired gravy or BECHAMEL SAUCE.

DESSERT SUGGESTIONS: Any kind of fresh, or canned fruit, chopped into small pieces. Reserved juice from canned fruit may be thickened with small amount of cornstarch and mixed with filling. Add a little coriander for extra flavor. Serve with WHIPPED TOPPING, VEGETARIAN CREAM, OR MAPLE WALNUT CREAM.

Entrees

OAT CREPES

¾ cup white flour
¾ cup whole wheat flour
1 ½ cup rolled oats
¾ teaspoon salt

Mix together and add:

4 cups soy milk (4 cups water to 1 cup soy milk powder)
1 tablespoon corn syrup

Let stand 5 minutes, then blend in blender until smooth.

Makes approximately 25 crepes

Chapter four

VEGETARIAN MEAT LOAF

1-8 ounce package bread stuffing mix
2 cups tofu, strained and crumbled
1 cup celery, sliced and sauteed
2 medium onions, chopped and sauteed
1 cup pecan meal
1 ½ cups hot water
1 ½ cups cooked, creamed celery or potato (can blend in blender after cooking to cream)
1 tablespoon McKay's Chicken Style Seasonning
 or 1 vegetable bullion cube dissolved in ¼ cup of water
1 ½ teaspoons onion powder
½ teaspoon garlic powder
¼ teaspoon sage

Mix all ingredients well. Press mixture into an oiled loaf pan and bake at 375 degrees for 45 minutes.

Serves 4

TOFU MEAT BALLS

Make one recipe of PECAN HERB LOAF, following instructions until time to bake. Rather than pressing into a loaf pan, form into balls. Bake at 350 degrees in an oiled baking dish for 35 minutes or until firm and brown. Serve over pasta and cover with SPAGHETTI SAUCE.

Makes about 18 balls

Entrees

TOSTADAS

2 onions, chopped
1 teaspoon garlic powder
2 cups tomatoes
1 tablespoon olive oil
2 teaspoons salt
8 cups cooked PINTO BEANS

Cook first four ingredients until nearly done. Add beans and salt and simmer 15 minutes. Blend to make paste. Pile in casserole serving dish and keep hot in oven. Serve over tostadas and top with chopped lettuce and tomatoes.

Serves 6

SHEPHERD PIE

2 cups cooked peas
2 cups onions, chopped and sauteed
2 cups carrots, diced and cooked until tender
2 cups Irish potato, chunked with peels on and cooked until tender
4 cups desired gravy
mashed potatoes for icing

Place all vegetables together in a deep casserole dish. Pour gravy over vegetables to fill about 1/3 of the dish. Spread mashed potatoes on top as icing. Heat in oven for about 30 minutes before serving.

Serves 4-6

Chapter four

PIZZA

1 clove garlic, minced
1 tablespoon olive oil
3/4 cup warm water
1 package dry yeast
1/4 teaspoon corn syrup
1 tablespoon olive oil
1 1/4 cup flour (white or whole wheat)
1/2 cup pastry flour (white or whole wheat)
1/2 teaspoon salt

Soak the garlic in the olive oil while you prepare the dough. In a large bowl, mix the warm water and yeast. Add the corn syrup and stir to dissolve. Add 1 tablespoon of olive oil and mix again. Mix the flours and salt. Slowly add the flour to the yeast mixture, stirring well. Roll the dough into a ball, turn out onto a lightly floured board, cover with a towel, and let stand for 10 minutes in a warm area. Knead the dough for about 10 minutes. Dough will become smooth and pliable. Form into a ball and place in a large oiled bowl, smooth side down. Roll it over to completely cover with oil. Cover with a damp towel, and let it rise in a warm place for 45 minutes. Preheat the oven to 450 degrees. Put dough in a 12-inch oiled pizza pan and gently push and press it into place, making a raised lip all around. Brush the dough with the garlic oil to prevent it from becoming soggy after the topping is added. Cover with your favorite toppings and bake for 20 minutes or until the crust starts to brown.

TOPPING SUGGESTIONS:
Cover dough with seasoned tomato sauce, then top with any of the following; sliced black olives, minced onion, minced green pepper, pineapple, chopped pieces of VEGETARIAN STEAKS.

Entrees

WALNUT BALLS

Mix:
6 cups steamed RICE
4 tablespoons nut butter
2 tablespoons soy flour

In saucepan stir together:
2 tablespoons oil
1 tablespoon flour
½ teaspoon onion salt

Add and stir in:
½ cup soy milk

Mix with above rice mixture

1 cup walnuts
½ cup celery
2 tablespoons onion, minced
2 tablespoons parsley flakes

Stir ingredients until well mixed. Chill until firm enough to hold shape. Using ice cream scoop form balls by packing and rounding mixture in the scoop. Roll each ball in seasoned bread crumbs. Place in shallow baking pans. Bake at 375 degrees for 45 minutes.

Chapter four

CHILI-N-GRITS

1 small onion, chopped
½ green pepper, chopped
1 tablespoon oil
1 teaspoon salt
1 teaspoon desired mixed herbs
1 cup uncooked corn grits
1 cup cooked red beans
4 cups water

Cook grits slowly in water with salt and herbs for two hours. Cook onion and green pepper in the oil until tender, then add to grits. Lower heat. Simmer 1 hour, stirring occasionally. Add cooked beans.

Serves 6

ITALIAN POTATO DUMPLINGS

2 pounds large baking potatoes
1 cup pastry flour (white or whole wheat)
½ teaspoon salt
2 cups pasta sauce of your choice

Steam the potatoes in their skins until tender. When they are cool enough to handle, peel and mash. Add the flour and salt. Knead on a lightly floured board until smooth. Sprinkle on a little more flour if the dough is sticky. Form into rolls about the thickness of your thumb. Cut into ¾-inch sections and press down lightly with a floured fork, (these are the dumplings). Bring a large pot of salted water to a boil. Add the dumplings and boil until they rise to the top. Drain and place in a warm bowl. Mix the dumplings with enough sauce to completely coat them.

Serves 4

Chapter four

COUNTRY BREAD STUFFING

1 cup chopped onion
1 cup celery, sliced thin
4 tablespoons oil
4 cups dry bread cubes
2 teaspoons salt
½ teaspoon garlic powder
½ teaspoon sage
1 teaspoon onion powder
Broth (amount will depend on your desired consistency)

Cook and stir onion and celery in oil until onion is tender. Stir in bread cubes. Add desired amount of water to moisten bread cubes. Place in a baking dish, and bake in oven at 325 degrees 40 minutes.

APPLE-RAISIN STUFFING: Add 1 ½ cups finely chopped apples and ½ cup raisins with remaining ingredients.

CORN STUFFING: Add 1 can (12 ounces) whole kernel corn, drained with remaining ingredients.

STUFFING BALLS: Shape stuffing by ½ cupfuls into balls; place in oiled baking dish. Cover and cook in oven at 325 degrees for 30 minutes. Uncover and cook 15 minutes longer.

Serves 4-6

STUFFED CABBAGE ROLLS

12-14 large cabbage leaves
1 ½ cups cabbage, grated small, steamed and drained
1 ½ cups cooked RICE
1 large onion, chopped and sauteed
2 stalks celery, sliced thin and sauteed
1 cup black olives, sliced
1 teaspoon salt
¼ teaspoon garlic powder
3 cups tomato sauce
½ teaspoon lemon juice

Cover cabbage with boiling water. Cover and let stand until leaves are limp, about 10 minutes. Remove leaves; drain. Mix rice, steamed cabbage, onion, celery, black olives, salt, garlic powder, and 1 ½ cups of the tomato sauce. Place about ⅓ cup of the mixture at stem end of each leaf. Roll leaf around mixture, tucking in sides. Place cabbage rolls seam sides down in oiled baking dish. Mix remaining tomato sauce and lemon juice; pour over cabbage rolls. Cover and cook in 350 degree oven for 30 to 45 minutes.

Serves 6-8

Chapter four

SUNFLOWER "BEEFY" POT PIE

CRUST
1 3/4 cup all-purpose flour
1/4 cup fine whole wheat flour
1 teaspoon salt
2/3 cup vegetable shortening
5 to 6 tablespoons cold water

FILLING
1/3 cup chopped celery
1/3 cup chopped potatoes
1/4 cup chopped carrots
1/4 cup frozen corn
1/4 cup frozen peas
3 tablespoons minced onion
1 teaspoon minced fresh parsley
3 tablespoon sunflower seeds
1 1/2 cups water
3/4 cup VEGETABLE STOCK
2 1/2 tablespoons cornstarch
1/2 teaspoon onion powder
1/2 teaspoon garlic powder
1/4 teaspoon salt
1 cup VEGETARIAN STEAKS, chopped small

Entrees

Heat oven to 400 degrees. For crust, combine flour, and salt in bowl. Cut in vegetable shortening until blended in to form pea size chunks. Sprinkle with water one tablespoon at a time. Toss lightly with fork until dough will form a ball. Divide dough into two parts. Press between hands to form two 5 to 6-inch "pancakes". Flour rolling surface and pin lightly. Roll dough for bottom crust into circle. Loosen dough carefully and place in pie plate. Moisten pastry edge with water. For filling, combine celery, potatoes, carrots, corn, peas, onion, parsley, sunflower seeds and 1 1/4 cups of the water in medium saucepan. Bring to a boil. Reduce heat and simmer for 10 minutes. Heat VEGETABLE STOCK in separate saucepan. Combine cornstarch, onion powder, garlic powder, salt and remaining 1/4 cup water in small bowl. Stir into VEGETABLE STOCK. Cook and stir until thickened. Add VEGETARIAN STEAKS, cooked vegetables and liquid. Spoon into unbaked pie shell. Roll top crust same as bottom and lift onto filled pie. Trim. Fold top edge under bottom crust. Flute with fork. Cut slits in top crust for steam to escape. Bake in oven at 400 degrees for 15 minutes. Reduce temperature to 350 degrees and bake for 20 to 25 minutes longer. Serve hot.

Serves 4-6

Chapter four

IRISH STEW

½ pound dried great northern beans
2 tablespoons vegetable oil
1 large onion, chopped
4 potatoes, sliced thin
3 carrots, sliced thin
4 cups cabbage, cut in chunks
Salt

Cook beans according to basic directions. Drain, reserving broth. Heat oil and saute onion, potatoes, and carrots until lightly browned. Add reserved bean broth and simmer until carrots are almost done. Add cabbage and cook 10 minutes longer. Add beans and salt. Cook 5 minutes.

Serves 4

VEGETABLE STEW

6-8 cups BROWN GRAVY
1 teaspoon salt
3 large potatoes, cut into medium sized cubes, boil until tender, then drain
3 medium carrots, peeled, sliced, boiled until tender, then drained
2 cups canned green beans
1 cup canned corn
2 stalks celery, sliced and sauteed until tender
2 large onions, chopped and sauteed until tender

Mix all cooked vegetables gently with gravy, then heat and serve.

Serves 4-6

Chapter four

GREAT NORTHERN STEW

½ pound great northern beans
¼ cup olive oil
3 cloves garlic, crushed
4 cups celery, cut in ½-inch pieces
1 head cauliflower cut into florets
2 cups cooked RICE
1 teaspoon oregano
Salt

Cook beans according to basic directions. Drain and reserve broth. Heat olive oil in large saucepan. Cook garlic in oil until lightly browned. Add celery and saute for 5 minutes. Add cauliflower and continue to saute another 5 minutes. Pour in reserved bean broth, cover pan, and simmer until vegetables are tender. Add beans, rice, oregano, and salt. Add water if needed to keep moist. Simmer 10 minutes.

Serves 4-6

Entrees

VEGETARIAN STEAKS

1 3/4 cups gluten flour
1/4 cup white flour
1/2 cup brewers yeast flakes
1 tablespoon wheat germ
1 package dry onion soup mix
1 3/4 - 2 1/4 cups hot tap water

Put all dry ingredients in a bowl and mix well. Add 1 3/4 cups of the hot tap water. Mixture will be sticky. Add enough of the remaining water to just moisten all dry ingredients. It is important to add only a little bit of water at a time. If too much water is added the dough will be too wet and will not boil into steaks, but will instead fall apart in the boiling broth. When mixture is ready to boil it will be a big sticky ball with an elastic consistency. Pull off medium size balls of dough and flatten with your fingers then drop into boiling broth and cook covered over medium heat 20-25 minutes. Remove from broth and chill overnight in a covered dish. These steaks can be used sliced into Chinese dishes, floured and fried in vegetable oil as steaks, or covered with Italian sauces and baked in the oven.

BROTH: Fill a very large pot 2/3 full of water, then add any of the following to season the broth: onion, carrot, celery, garlic powder, vegex, salt, parsley, soy sauce, potatoes.

Chapter four

BAKED VEGI-BURGERS

4 ½ cups water
½ cup soy sauce
4 ½ cups old-fashioned oats
⅓ cup oil (Optional)
1 diced onion
1 teaspoon basil
3 cloves garlic, crushed
¼ cup yeast flakes
¼ cup sesame seeds
¾ cup sunflower seeds
½ cup dry bread crumbs

Cook oats, onion, basil, and garlic in boiling water and soy sauce for about 5 minutes. Stir constantly to keep from scorching. Mix remaining ingredients in a separate bowl. Add dry ingredients to cooked oats and mix well. When cool enough to handle, form into patties and bake at 350 degrees for 30-45 minutes (turn after 15-20 minutes) until nicely browned on each side.

Makes approximately 8-10 burgers 1 inch thick.

NOTE: Oil is not necessary in these burgers, but it does make the burgers stay moist longer if they are being kept for later use.

TOFU BURGERS

1 pound firm Chinese tofu
1/4 cup soy flour
2 tablespoons flour (white or whole wheat)
2 tablespoons cornstarch
1/2 teaspoons garlic powder
3 tablespoons soy sauce
1/4 small onion, minced
2 tablespoons vegetable oil

Drain the tofu. Wrap in a clean non-terry kitchen towel and wring out excess water. Tofu will crumble. Combine the soy flour, whole wheat flour, cornstarch, and garlic powder and mix well. Mix the tofu, soy sauce, and onion. Add the dry ingredients and mix well. Knead with your hands until all ingredients are well blended and mixture holds together. Let stand 20 minutes. Form into patties. Heat the oil in a skillet. Add the patties, and over medium heat, cook for 7 minutes. Turn over and cook for 7 minutes more.

Makes 4 large patties

Chapter four

SPLIT PEA PATTIES

2 1/2 cups cooked SPLIT PEAS (cooked thick)
1/2 medium onion, minced
1 cup fine, dry bread crumbs
1/3 cup water
1/2 teaspoon salt
1/4 cup flour

Mash split peas with a fork. Mix all ingredients. Shape into patties. Bake at 350 degrees until browned on both sides.

Makes about 5 patties

Entrees

SAVORY MILLET PATTIES

2 cups millet
8 cups water
2 teaspoons onion powder
2 teaspoons garlic powder
1 teaspoon Italian seasoning
1 teaspoon sweet basil
2 cups dry bread crumbs
½ cup brewers yeast flakes
2 tablespoons sesame seeds

Put first 6 ingredients in a cooking pot. Bring to a boil, then reduce heat to medium-low and simmer covered until millet has soaked up all of the water (about 45 minutes). Stir occasionally, especially during last 15-20 minutes to keep from burning. When done cooking, remove from heat and let stand uncovered for 15 minutes to cool slightly. Add remaining ingredients and mix well. Form into patties ½" thick. Place patties on a lightly oiled cookie sheet. Bake at 350 degrees for 30 minutes, turning after 15 minutes.

Makes 14-16 patties

Chapter four

OAT BURGERS OR LOAF

2 cups cooked oatmeal
1 raw potato, grated
½ cup onion, chopped
1-2 cups bread crumbs
1 teaspoon salt
½ teaspoon sage
2 tablespoons oil

Grind potato, onion, and oil in blender. Use a little water in blender if needed. Mix with cooked oatmeal. Add remaining items and mix. Use more crumbs if water used in blender. Form patties or make into roast. Bake at 350 degrees in oiled tin until nicely browned. Burgers require 45 minutes, turning after 30 minutes. Loaf requires about 60 minutes.

Serves 4

Entrees

SUN PATTIES

½ pound dried chick-peas
1 cup sunflower seeds
1 tablespoon lemon juice
2 tablespoons flour
½ medium onion, chopped
1 small clove garlic, crushed
¼ teaspoon cumin
Salt
1 cup or more bread crumbs
Olive oil

Cook chick-peas according to basic directions on package. Drain, reserving broth. Put into blender, in batches, sunflower seeds, chick-peas, lemon juice, onion, garlic, salt, cumin, and just enough reserved bean broth to blend ingredients. Blend a few seconds. Pour into a bowl and stir. Add bread crumbs and flour, mix well. Form into 3 inch patties. Dust each with flour mixed with a dash of salt. Fry in olive oil until golden brown on both sides, or bake in oven at 350 until browned.

Serves 4

Chapter four

CASHEW GARBANZO BAKE

1 cup celery, chopped
1 cup onion, chopped
½ cup black olives, sliced
2 tablespoons oil
1 cup cashews, chopped
2 cups cooked GARBANZOS
2 cups rolled oats
2 teaspoons salt
2 cups water

Saute celery and onion in oil until slightly tender. Whirl ½ of the GARBANZOS in blender with enough water or broth to turn blender easily. Mix all ingredients. Bake in greased casserole dish at 350 degrees for about 1 hour.

Serves 4

CREOLE

1 teaspoon oil
1 1/4 cup onion, diced
2 tomatoes, peeled and diced
2 teaspoons salt
1 bay leaf
1/2 cup tomato sauce
3 cups cooked GARBANZOS

Saute onion in a large skillet over low heat until tender. Add tomatoes, salt, bay leaf, and tomato sauce. Cover and simmer 15 minutes. Add garbanzos. Cover and simmer 10 minutes longer. Serve over hot cooked RICE.

Serves 6

GARBANZO POT PIE

3 cups cooked GARBANZOS
4 cups CASHEW GRAVY
4 potatoes, peeled, cubed, boiled and drained
4 stalks celery, sliced and sauteed
1 medium onion, chopped and sauteed

Mix together all ingredients then place in a baking dish. Cover with desired pie crust. Bake at 350 degrees for about 1 hour.

Serves 6

Chapter four

MEXICAN GARBANZOS

4 cups cooked GARBANZOS
1 onion, chopped small
1 green bell pepper, minced
2 tablespoons olive oil
3 clove of garlic, minced
3 cup tomato sauce
2 tablespoons molasses
Salt as needed

Saute the onion, green pepper, and garlic in olive oil until slightly tender. Add remaining ingredients and pour into the garbanzos. Cook over medium-low heat 30-60 minutes.

Serves 4-6

EAST INDIA BLACK-EYED PEAS

3 cups water
1 cup dry black-eyed peas
1 large onion, chopped
2 tablespoons coconut
$1/2$ teaspoons paprika
1 teaspoon corn syrup
Salt to taste

Soak peas in water 2 hours or overnight. Boil in soaking water until tender. Add remaining ingredients and cook 10 to 20 minutes longer to blend flavors.

Serves 2-4

Entrees

BAKED BEANS

4 cups cooked NAVY BEANS
2 cups canned tomatoes
1 tablespoon salt
1 ½ cups tomato sauce
¼ cup molasses
½ tablespoons sweet basil
1 ½ cups onion, chopped

Mix all ingredients well. Put into covered baking dish and bake at 350 degrees for 45 minutes.

Serves 4-6

Chapter four

BEANS AND PASTA

½ pound dried white beans
4 cups VEGETABLE STOCK
2 teaspoons olive oil
2 cloves garlic, crushed
1 small onion, finely chopped
1 cup tomato sauce
¼ teaspoon basil
Salt to taste
2 celery stalks, sliced thin
½ pound spaghetti broken into 2-inch pieces

Boil the beans and celery in the broth for 3 minutes. Let them stand for 1 ½ hours. In a saucepan heat the olive oil and saute the garlic and onion until tender. Add the tomato sauce and basil. Bring to a boil and simmer for 10 minutes. Combine this sauce with the celery and beans in their soaking liquid and simmer until the beans are tender. Add seasonings if desired. Cook the pasta, drain, and mix with the beans.

Serves 4

BLACK-EYED PEA POTPOURRI

1 pound dried black-eyed peas
2 cloves garlic, crushed
2 carrots, sliced
8 stalks celery, sliced
1 tablespoon olive oil
1 28-ounce can tomatoes, chopped
1 8-ounce can tomato sauce
2 bay leaves
Salt

Cook black-eyed peas according to basic directions. Drain, reserving broth. Saute garlic, carrots, and celery in olive oil for 5 minutes. Add tomatoes, tomato sauce, bay leaves, and black-eyed pea broth. Cook until vegetables are tender. Add black-eyed peas and salt. Cook 10 minutes longer. This is nice served over hot BROWN RICE or bulgar.

Serves 6-8

Chapter four

LIMA BEAN AND TOMATO CASSEROLE

1 pound dry lima beans
2 cups canned tomatoes
½ cup celery, sliced thin
2 onions, sliced into thin rings
2 tablespoons oil
2 teaspoons sugar
1 teaspoon salt

Soak the washed beans overnight then boil them in the water they soaked in until tender. Add remaining ingredients and place in a casserole dish. Add more water if necessary and bake at 300 degrees for 1 hour.

Serves 4-6

CHILI

4 cups cooked pinto beans
2 cups tomato juice
2 small onions, minced
1 green pepper, cleaned and chopped
¾ teaspoon salt
3 teaspoons cumin
2 cloves of garlic, crushed
1 cup VEGETARIAN STEAKS chopped into small pieces (optional)

Mix all ingredients in large pot and cook over medium heat for 30 minutes stirring frequently. Serve with CRACKERS.

Serves 4

REFRIED BEANS

2 cups water
8 ounces dried pinto beans (about 1 1/4 cups)
1 medium onion, chopped
1/4 cup oil
3/4 teaspoon salt

Mix water, beans, and onion in 2-quart saucepan. Cover and heat to boiling; boil 2 minutes. Remove from heat and let stand for 1 hour. Add just enough water to cover beans. Heat to boiling; reduce heat. Cover and boil gently, stirring occasionally, until beans are very tender, about 2 hours. Mash beans. Stir in oil and salt, and cook slowly in a cast iron skillet for 5-10 minutes, stirring often.

Serves 4-6

Chapter four

BLACK BEANS

4 cups cooked BLACK BEANS
   (and 4 cups of liquid beans were cooked in)
2 cups onions, chopped and sauteed
1 green pepper, chopped and sauteed
¼ cup soy sauce
2 cloves of garlic, crushed

OPTIONAL ADDITIONS: sliced sauteed zucchini and/or summer squash

Mix all ingredients and cook over medium heat for 30 minutes. If adding zucchini or squash, put sliced squash in with beans 10 minutes before serving and cook over medium heat just until squash is tender. Serve over hot cooked RICE.

Serves 4-6

BEANS AND GREENS

1 pound dried great northern beans
2 large bunches greens
2/3 cup olive oil
4 large cloves garlic, halved
1/2 cup peeled and chopped tomatoes
1 teaspoon oregano
Salt

Cook beans according to basic directions. Pick over greens, wash thoroughly, and cut into 3 inch lengths. Blanch the greens in a large pot of boiling, lightly salted water, then drain greens and set aside. There should be at least 3 cups of blanched greens. Heat olive oil in a saucepan. Add garlic cloves and brown on both sides. Remove 1/2 the garlic-oil mixture and set aside. In the remaining oil and garlic, cook tomatoes for 2 minutes. Add greens and salt; cook until greens are tender. Add reserved oil, garlic, oregano, salt, and greens to cooked drained beans. Cook 5 to 10 minutes longer.

Serves 6

Chapter four

LIMA BROCCOLI BAKE

½ pound dried baby lima beans
Salt
1 bunch broccoli, cut into small pieces
2 tablespoons oil
3 tablespoons flour
2 cups hot soy milk

Cook beans according to basic directions. Drain beans and place them in a 2-quart casserole dish. Sprinkle with salt. Steam broccoli for 5 minutes, drain, then place evenly over beans. In saucepan, heat oil over low heat. Blend in flour and cook for 1 minute, stirring constantly. Add soy milk all at once and bring to a boil while stirring. When smooth add salt to taste. Pour the sauce over the beans and broccoli. Sprinkle with bread crumbs. Bake in oven at 350 degrees until casserole is bubbling, about 30 minutes.

Serves 4

SPLIT PEAS AND RICE CASSEROLE

3 cups cooked SPLIT PEAS
2 cups cooked RICE
2 cups canned tomatoes
½ cup onion, minced
Salt to taste
Bread crumbs

In greased baking dish make layers of peas, rice, tomatoes, and onion. Sprinkle with salt if needed, cover top with bread crumbs. Bake at 400 degrees for 20 minutes.

Serves 6

LENTIL-NUT ROAST

3 cups cooked LENTILS
½ cup ground sunflower seeds
1 tablespoon onion powder
¼ teaspoon sage
1 teaspoon salt
½ cup rolled oats or bread crumbs

Mix all ingredients well, using water to adjust consistency so that oats are quite wet. Bake in oiled loaf pan for 1 hour at 350 degrees. Serve with CASHEW GRAVY.

Serves 2-4

Chapter four

SWEET AND SOUR LENTILS

½ pound dried lentils
½ cup water or VEGETABLE STOCK
⅓ cup apple juice
¼ cup lemon juice
1 ½ tablespoons sugar
1 tablespoon blackstrap molasses
2 bay leaves
1 tablespoon chopped scallions
Salt

Cook lentils according to basic directions. In a small saucepan, dissolve 3 vegetable bouillon cubes in water. Add apple juice, lemon juice, sugar, molasses, bay leaves, and scallions. Boil 2 minutes. Combine sauce with drained lentils. Add salt and cook until hot and bubbling.

Serves 4

Entrees

ITALIAN LENTILS

2 ½ cups dry lentils
1 - 15 ounce can tomato sauce
1 onion, chopped
1 green pepper, cleaned and chopped
2 cloves garlic, minced
¾ teaspoon salt
¼ teaspoon oregano
1 teaspoon Italian seasoning
1 teaspoon olive oil

Cook lentils in boiling salted water until tender; drain. Saute onions, green pepper, and garlic in olive oil until onions and pepper are tender. Mix lentils, tomato sauce, and seasonings. Stir in onions, pepper, and garlic. Put into casserole dish and bake at 350 degrees for 30-40 minutes. Top with dry bread crumbs if desired.

Serves 4-6

Chapter four

LENTILS AND NOODLES

2 teaspoons vegetable oil
1 large onion, chopped
1 cup water
2 cups cooked LENTILS
5 large ripe tomatoes, chopped
1 cup black olives, sliced
1 teaspoon salt
3 cups elbow macaroni, cooked and drained

Heat the oil in the bottom of a large pot. Add the onion and cook until tender. Add the water, salt, lentils, tomatoes and their juices. Bring to a boil and cook, covered, for 10 minutes, stirring often. Add macaroni and black olives, and cook over medium heat for 10 minutes, stirring occasionally.

Serves 4-6

Entrees

LENTIL CASSEROLE

1 pound lentils, cooked and drained
5 medium potatoes, peeled, cubed, boiled until tender, and drained
3 carrots, sliced, cooked, and drained
1 medium onion, chopped and sauteed
3 stalks celery, sliced and sauteed
1 teaspoon salt
1 teaspoon celery salt
2 ½ cups BROWN GRAVY

Put all ingredients in a casserole dish and mix well. Top with bread crumbs if desired. Bake in oven at 350 degrees for 30-40 minutes.

Serves 4-6

Chapter four

CHINESE PEPPER STEAK

2 1/2 cups fresh broccoli, use only the flowering parts, no stems
1 large green bell pepper sliced into thin wedges
1/2 small red bell pepper sliced into thin wedges
2 medium onions, peeled and cut into wedges
1 large carrot, peeled and sliced thin
3 small tomatoes, sliced into wedges
4 cups VEGETARIAN STEAKS, cut into 1/2 wide strips
6 cups water
6 tablespoons cornstarch
8 tablespoons soy sauce
1/2 teaspoon garlic powder
1 teaspoon onion powder

Put water, soy sauce, garlic powder, and onion powder in large cooking pot and bring to a boil. In the meantime mix cornstarch with a small amount of water, add to pot when mixture boils. Cook until thick and bubbly, then turn heat down to medium (if a thicker sauce is desired, add more cornstarch, if too bland, add more soy sauce). Add VEGETARIAN STEAKS, broccoli, carrots, and onions. Cook over medium heat for 10 minutes. Add peppers, cook 5 minutes more. Add tomatoes and serve immediately over hot cooked RICE.

Serves 4-6

Entrees

SUKIYAKI

⅓ cup soy sauce
2 tablespoons sugar
2 tablespoons vegetable oil
1 teaspoon onion powder
½ teaspoon garlic powder
½ cup boiling water
8 green salad onions, cut into 1 inch pieces
2 large onions, thinly sliced
3 medium stalks celery, cut into diagonal slices
1 can (8 ½ ounces) bamboo shoots, drained
3 cups spinach, torn into bite-size pieces

In a large skillet, heat oil, add onions and celery, saute for 2 minutes over medium heat. Add remaining ingredients, cover and simmer for 10 to 15 minutes.

Serves 4

Chapter four

VEGETABLE CHOW MEIN

1 onion, chopped large
2 teaspoons oil
3 cups shredded cabbage
1 1/2 cups broccoli, cut into small pieces
8 ounces water chestnuts, sliced
8 ounces bamboo shoots
8 ounces mung bean sprouts
1 cup frozen pea pods, thawed
1/3 cup soy sauce
1/4 cup cornstarch

Steam broccoli in 2 cups of water until tender, drain, reserving juice. In large skillet, cook onions and cabbage with oil until tender-crisp. In small dish mix cornstarch into broth from broccoli and soy sauce. Add to onions and cabbage along with remaining ingredients. Cook over medium heat until hot stirring frequently.

Serves 4

JAMBALAYA

2 teaspoons vegetable oil
1 large onion, minced
2 cloves garlic, minced
1 medium green pepper, cleaned and chopped
1 stalk celery, sliced thin
2 1/2 cups canned tomatoes, chopped
1 cup uncooked rice
2 1/2 cups water
1/2 teaspoon thyme
3 tablespoons soy sauce
1/2 teaspoon cumin

Heat the oil in a large skillet. Add the onion and cook until golden. Add the garlic, green pepper, and celery and cook until the pepper is tender. Preheat the oven to 350 degrees. Add all remaining ingredients and mix well. Place the mixture in an oiled casserole dish. Cover and bake for 2 hours or until the rice is done.

Serves 6

Chapter four

CASHEW RICE ROAST

3 ½ cups cooked RICE
1 ½ cups cashew pieces, ground
2 ½ cups soy milk
1 ½ cups onion, chopped
¾ teaspoons garlic powder
2 ½ tablespoons McKay's Chicken Style Seasoning (optional)
2 ½ tablespoons parsley flakes
½ tablespoons salt
1 ¼ teaspoons onion powder

Gently mix all ingredients together. Put rice mixture in casserole dish. Bake at 350 degrees for 1 hour.

Serves 4

FRIED RICE

2 cups cooked RICE
1 tablespoon soy sauce
1 tablespoon oil
3/4 cup vegetable broth, or broth made from McKay's seasoning
1/2 cup sliced green onion
1/2 cup finely shredded cabbage
1 small carrot, peeled and chopped fine

Mix all ingredients, and cook over medium heat until broth has been soaked up. Stir often to prevent burning.

Serves 2-4

HOPPIN' JOHN

1 cup dry black-eyed peas
8 cups VEGETABLE STOCK or water
1 cup uncooked rice
1 1/2 teaspoons salt

Wash and drain peas. Put peas and broth in a kettle. Boil 2 minutes. Remove from heat, cover, and let stand 1 hour. Add salt. Boil gently 1-2 hours until peas are almost tender. Add rice. Do not stir after this time. Cover and boil gently about 60 minutes, until rice is tender.

Serves 2-4

Chapter four

SPANISH RICE

1 large onion, chopped
2/3 cup chopped green pepper
3 tablespoons olive oil
2 1/2 cups water
1 cup uncooked rice
1 can (16 ounces) stewed tomatoes
1 cup tomato sauce
1/2 cup frozen peas
1/2 cup frozen corn
1 teaspoon cumin
1/2 teaspoon dried oregano leaves
1 1/4 teaspoon salt

Saute onion and green pepper in 3 tablespoons of oil until tender. Stir in remaining ingredients. Heat to boiling; reduce heat. Cover and simmer, stirring occasionally, until rice is tender, about 30 minutes. Add a small amount of water during cooking if necessary.

Serves 4-6

Entrees

RICE MEDLEY

1 1/2 cups canned peas, or frozen peas thawed
1 carrot, peeled and shredded
1 cup pearl onions
1 1/2 cups uncooked rice
1/2 teaspoon salt

Pour 3 cups water into a 2-quart saucepan. Heat to boiling. Stir in peas, carrot, onions, rice, and salt. Heat to boiling again, reduce heat to low and simmer for 20 to 30 minutes.

Serves 4

CARROT RICE LOAF

2 cups grated raw carrots
4 cups cooked RICE
1 cup bread crumbs
1 cup onion, chopped and sauteed
1 tablespoon onion powder
1 1/2 teaspoon salt
1/2 teaspoon thyme
1/2 teaspoon garlic powder
3 cups BECHAMEL SAUCE

Mix all ingredients well. Bake in casserole dish uncovered at 350 degrees for 40 minutes.

Serves 4-6

Chapter four

MACARONI AND CHEE

4 cups macaroni, cooked and drained
1 cup onion, chopped and sauteed
1/2 teaspoons garlic powder
1/2 teaspoon salt
1 cup black olives, sliced
2 1/4 cups CHEE SAUCE

Mix all ingredients well and turn into oiled casserole dish. Bake at 350 degrees for 30-40 minutes.

Serves 4

BAKED MACARONI

6 cups macaroni, cooked and drained
2 cloves garlic, minced
2 green peppers, chopped
2 large onions, chopped
2 tablespoons olive oil
1 teaspoon salt

Saute garlic, peppers, and onions in olive oil until tender, then mix into cooked noodles. Add salt, mix. Pour into a casserole dish, cover top with bread crumbs, and bake in oven at 400 degrees for 15 minutes or until hot.

Serves 6

CABBAGE CASSEROLE

8 ounces flat pasta
1 tablespoon olive oil
1 medium onion, sliced
1 medium head cabbage, cored and sliced 1/2 inch thick
1/2 teaspoon celery seeds
2 1/2 cups water
3 tablespoons flour
1 1/2 cups sliced celery
1 1/2 cups sliced carrots
bread crumbs

Cook noodles in boiling salted water until almost done. Drain and set aside. Cook celery and carrots in boiling salted water until carrots are tender. Place cooked vegetables in a blender with just enough water to make blender move vegetables around. Blend until creamy, then set aside. In a large saucepan, heat the olive oil over medium heat; add the onion and cook, uncovered, until soft. Add the cabbage and celery seeds and cook for 1 minute. Add 1/2 cup of the water, cover, and simmer until the cabbage is tender. In a small bowl, whisk together the remaining water and the flour. Add to the cabbage, reduce heat to medium low, and cook, stirring until slightly thickened. Add the creamed celery and carrots. Stir in the noodles. Pour mixture into an ungreased shallow casserole, sprinkle with bread crumbs, and bake uncovered for 30-35 minutes or until bubbling and browned on top.

Serves 4-6

Chapter four

GOULASH

1 can (16 ounces) whole tomatoes
1 teaspoon salt
1/4 teaspoon dried oregano leaves
1/2 teaspoon basil
1/2 cup black olives, sliced
2 cups uncooked macaroni

Chop tomatoes, reserving liquid, then heat tomatoes and their liquid, 1 teaspoon salt, oregano, and basil to boiling. Reduce heat and simmer uncovered, stirring occasionally, 10 to 12 minutes. Cook macaroni in boiling salted water until tender; drain. Arrange noodles in serving dish; pour sauce on hot macaroni and sprinkle with sliced olives. Garnish with parsley sprigs.

Serves 2-4

Entrees

GARBANZOS AND PASTA

1 pound dry garbanzo's
12 ounces Rotini Twist Macaroni
2 bay leaves
1 ½ teaspoons sweet basil flakes
1 teaspoon savory
2 teaspoons onion powder
3 large cloves garlic, crushed
1 large onion, chopped

Place all ingredients except Rotini in a large cooking pot. Cover with 4" water. Bring to a boil for 2 minutes, then remove from heat and cover. Let stand overnight. Return to a boil, then reduce heat to medium and cook for 4-5 hours or until garbanzos are soft, but not overcooked. More water may be needed during cooking. Add 2 teaspoons of salt during last hour of cooking. When garbanzo's are finished, turn heat to low and let set while cooking pasta. Cook pasta in separate pot in boiling salted water until tender. Drain and add to garbanzo's.

Serves 6-8

Chapter four

PEPPERS AND PASTA

2 teaspoons olive oil
1 onion, quartered and sliced
3 garlic cloves, crushed
3 sweet red peppers, cleaned and cut into thin strips
3 green bell peppers, cleaned and cut into thin strips
1 ½ tablespoons soy sauce
16 ounce can stewed tomatoes, chop tomatoes, reserve liquid
1 pound pasta of choice, cooked in boiling salted water until tender then drained

In a large skillet heat the oil. Add the onion and cook over medium heat until the onion is light brown. Add the garlic, peppers, and soy sauce and cook, covered for 10 minutes. Add the tomatoes and their liquid. Cook, covered over low heat for 30 minutes. Serve over pasta.

Serves 4

FRI CHIC AND PASTA

2 large onions, chopped into large pieces
4 cloves garlic, crushed
1 - 6 ounce can pitted olives, drain and slice olives in half
1 pound Fri Chic (by Worthington), or use 2 cups VEGETARIAN STEAKS, cut into bite size pieces
2 - 30 ounce cans tomato sauce
2 teaspoons savory
2 teaspoons oregano
2 teaspoons basil
16 ounces Gnocchi (pasta) or medium size shell pasta
½ cup bread crumbs

Saute onions, garlic, and seasonings in 3 tablespoons olive oil until onions are tender. Add tomato sauce and simmer 30 minutes. Stir often. While sauce simmers, cook pasta in salted boiling water until nearly done. Drain. Add pasta, sliced olives, and Fri Chic to sauce and mix well. Pour pasta mixture into casserole dish. Cover with bread crumbs. Bake at 350 degrees for 20-30 minutes or until bubbly.

Serves 6

Chapter four

PASTA PRIMAVERA

1 clove garlic, thinly sliced
1 tablespoon olive oil
1 pound curly pasta
1/4 cup green beans
1/2 cup VEGETABLE STOCK
2 carrots, sliced thin
1 yellow crookneck squash, halved lengthwise and sliced
1 cup cauliflower florets, small
1 cup broccoli florets, small
1/2 cup fresh peas
1/4 teaspoon salt

Soak the garlic in the olive oil for 15 minutes. Cook pasta in boiling salted water until tender, then drain. In a large skillet, heat the stock. Add the carrots, squash, cauliflower, broccoli, peas, and salt. Cover and cook for 5 minutes or until the vegetables are tender. Place the freshly drained noodles in a large warm bowl, add the cooked vegetables and garlic oil (discarding garlic slices first), and toss.

Serves 4-6

Entrees

STUFFED MANICOTTI

2 teaspoons olive oil
1 small onion, minced
1/4 green pepper, minced
1/4 teaspoon marjoram
1 teaspoon basil
3 large cloves garlic, crushed
1 large zucchini, diced
1 cup canned spinach, drained and chopped
2 tablespoons fresh parsley, chopped
1 1/2 cups canned tomatoes, drained and chopped
1 teaspoon salt
1 pound firm tofu
2 tablespoons olive oil
1/2 teaspoon salt
dash coriander
2 teaspoons lemon juice
10-12 manicotti shells
4 cups tomato sauce or SPAGHETTI SAUCE

Heat 2 teaspoons olive oil in a large skillet. Add onion, marjoram, and basil. Cook, covered, until the onion is tender. Add the garlic and cook for 1 minute more. Add green pepper and zucchini, cover and cook over medium heat for 5 minutes. Add the parsley, tomatoes, and salt. Cook, covered for 10 minutes longer. Remove cover, stir in spinach and continue cooking until all liquid is cooked out of vegetables. Place the tofu, 1/2 teaspoon of salt, and lemon juice in a blender and blend until smooth. Stir into vegetables. Preheat the oven to 350 degrees. Fill each shell with tofu/vegetable mixture. Pour 1/2 inch of tomato sauce in the bottom of baking dish. Set the manicotti shells side by side in the dish, cover with sauce. Bake covered for 20 minutes. Remove cover and continue to bake until sauce begins to bubble.

Serves 4-6

Chapter four

LASAGNA

1 large onion, chopped
2 cloves garlic, pressed
2 cans (16 ounces) whole tomatoes
2 cans (15 ounces) tomato sauce
2 tablespoons dried parsley flakes
2 teaspoons dried basil leaves
1 1/2 teaspoon dried oregano leaves
1 pound tofu, strained and crumbled
1 teaspoon salt
1 1/2 cups cooked spinach, drained and chopped
15 uncooked lasagna noodles
CHEE SAUCE (optional)

Cook noodles in boiling, salted water until tender but not falling apart. Drain, then rinse in cold water. In the meantime saute onion and garlic in 2 tablespoons vegetable oil until tender. Add tomatoes (with liquid), tomato sauce, parsley, basil, oregano, and salt. Simmer 20 minutes over medium-low heat stirring occasionally. Layer 1/3 each of the noodles, sauce, tofu, and spinach in ungreased 13x9x2 oblong pan. Repeat 2 times. Spoon any remaining sauce on top layer of noodles along with CHEE SAUCE if desired. Cook uncovered in 350 degrees oven for 45 minutes. Let stand 10 minutes before cutting.

Serves 6-8

VEGETABLE LASAGNA

2 large onions, chopped in large pieces, and sauteed until tender
3 cups broccoli florets (small pieces), steamed until tender
3 medium carrots, peeled, sliced thin, and boiled until tender
2 small green peppers, cleaned, chopped, and sauteed
2 cups black olives, sliced
2 can (16 ounces each) canned tomatoes, chopped
3 cans (15 ounces each) tomato sauce
4 cloves garlic, pressed
2 tablespoons parsley flakes
2 teaspoons dried basil
1 ½ teaspoon salt
2 teaspoons dried oregano leaves
1 teaspoon Italian seasoning
15 lasagna noodles, cooked, drained, and rinsed in cold water

Make sauce with crushed tomatoes, tomato sauce, pressed garlic, parsley flakes, dried basil, salt, oregano and Italian seasoning. Simmer while lasagna noodles are cooking. To assemble lasagna, on the bottom of an oblong baking pan place 3 or 4 noodles. Top with sauce, then add ½ of each; onions, broccoli, carrots, green peppers, and black olives, spreading evenly across first layer of noodles and sauce. Repeat one more time, then cover with third layer of noodles. Top with remaining sauce. Bake in oven at 350 degrees for 30 minutes or until sauce is bubbly.

Serves 6-8

Gravies and Sauces

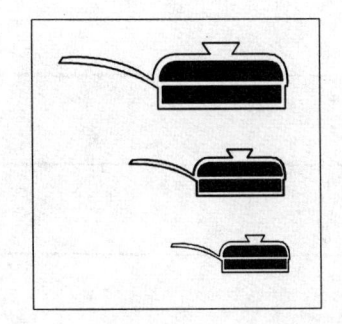

GRAVIES AND SAUCES

Basic Gravy	159
Bean Gravy	159
Bechamel Sauce	165
Brown Gravy	160
Cashew Gravy	160
Creamy Onion Gravy	161
Garlic Tomato Sauce	167
Holiday Gravy	161
Italian Tomato Sauce	169
Mrs. Tyler's Gravy	162
Onion Sauce	166
Sauteed Gravy	162
Seasoned Gravy	163

Seasoned Tomato Sauce	167
Spaghetti Sauce	168
Sunflower Gravy	164
Sweet and Sour Sauce	164
Tomato Relish	166
White Sauce	165

Chapter Five

GRAVIES AND SAUCES

Gravies and sauces may be subtly flavored and served with roasts, patties, or souffles. The purpose of gravies and sauces is to enhance the flavors of the dish it accompanies, not to cover up or alter.

If the basic sauces are learned, it is easy to become proficient in making many good sauces. To make masterpieces of simple dishes requires only a light touch with the oil, the onion, the flour, the broth, and the seasonings.

One must learn to make a roux, blending and lightly browning the flour. Slowly add the liquid, and stir continuously. Simmer 3 or 4 minutes over a very low heat to cook the flour. Never have sauces too thick, and never have so much that the food is swimming in it.

Gravies can be thickened with flour or cornstarch. Cornstarch has about twice the thickening power as that of flour. As a general rule, use 2 tablespoons of flour for each cup of liquid, or use 1 tablespoon of cornstarch for each cup of liquid.

BASIC GRAVY

4 cups water
8 tablespoons flour
1 teaspoon salt

Place flour and 2 cups of the water in a covered plastic container. Shake until smooth. Put the flour mixture, remaining water and salt into medium saucepan. Cook gently until thick. Reduce heat and simmer for 20 minutes stirring occasionally. Season with any of the following:

Soy Sauce
McKay's Chicken or Beef style seasoning
Kitchen Bouquet
Vegetable broth can be used in place of the water

Serves 4

BEAN GRAVY

Use any leftover beans. Place 1-2 cups in blender with enough water to make the desired consistency. Season with onion or garlic, salt, and herbs of choice.

Chapter Five

BROWN GRAVY

4 tablespoons oil
6 tablespoons white flour
4 cups hot water
2 teaspoons kitchen bouquet
1 teaspoon dried basil
1 1/2 teaspoons salt

Heat oil in saucepan. Slowly add flour mixing with oil. Add water and thicken. Add kitchen bouquet and salt. Cook over medium heat for 5 minutes stirring frequently.

Makes about 4 cups

CASHEW GRAVY

2 cups water
1/4 cup cashews
2 tablespoons cornstarch
1/2 teaspoon salt
1 teaspoon onion powder

Place 1 cup of the water and cashews in blender and blend until smooth. Add remaining ingredients and blend again until well mixed. Place mixture in small saucepan and cook over medium heat until thick and bubbly, stirring constantly.

Makes about 2 cups

Gravies and Sauces

CREAMY ONION GRAVY

2 tablespoons vegetable oil
2 tablespoons flour
1 cup soy milk
½ cup onions, sliced and sauteed

Heat vegetable oil in saucepan. Stir in flour. Cook over low heat, stirring constantly, until mixture is smooth and bubbly. Stir in soy milk. Heat to boiling. Boil and stir one minute. Add onions and serve over hot cooked rice or mashed potatoes.

Makes about 1 ½ cups

HOLIDAY GRAVY

3 cups water
½ cup flour, dextrinized
2 tablespoons oil
1 tablespoon food yeast
1 teaspoon salt

Place flour in dry pan in oven at 300 degrees for about 10 to 15 minutes to lightly brown (DEXTRINIZE). Mix all ingredients in a blender, then pour mixture into a saucepan and cook until thick and bubbly. Cover and simmer for about 10 minutes. If a thinner gravy is desired add a little more water.

Makes about 3 cups

Chapter Five

SAUTEED GRAVY

After sauteing any vegetable, remove the vegetable and add flour to the oil in the pan in the proportion of about 3:1. Roast the flour and add any vegetable stock or soy milk to the desired consistency for gravy. Add salt and seasonings to desired flavor, simmer until serving time, stirring occasionally.

MRS. TYLER'S GRAVY

1 cup whole wheat flour
3 tablespoons vegetable oil
1 quart water
½ cup soy sauce
1 teaspoon onion powder
½ teaspoon Italian seasoning
½ teaspoon salt

Brown flour in skillet, then add oil. Mix together well, then add water and soy sauce. Stir constantly over medium heat until thick and bubbly. Continue to cook for 5 minutes over low heat, stirring occasionally.

Makes about 4 cups

SEASONED GRAVY

2 cups water
1/4 cup flour
1/2 teaspoon salt
1 teaspoon onion powder
1/4 teaspoon crushed bay leaf

Put flour and 1 cup of the water into a small covered plastic container and shake until smooth. Put flour mixture into a small saucepan with remaining water and seasonings. Cook until thick stirring frequently.

Makes about 2 cups

Chapter Five

SUNFLOWER GRAVY

½ cup sunflower seeds
4 tablespoons cornstarch
¼ cup brewers yeast flakes
2 cloves fresh garlic, peeled
1 teaspoon onion powder
½ teaspoon sweet basil flakes
1 teaspoon salt

Place all ingredients in blender with 1 cup of water. Blend until thick and creamy, about 1 minute. Add one more cup of water and blend for 2 minutes. Pour mixture into cooking pot, add 2 cups water, bring to a boil, reduce heat to medium-low and cook 20-30 minutes. Stir often. If a thinner gravy is desired add more water.

Makes about 4 cups

SWEET AND SOUR SAUCE

In saucepan mix ¾ cup corn syrup, ½ cup lemon juice, ½ cup water, 1 tablespoon chopped green pepper, and ½ teaspoon salt. Simmer 5 minutes. Combine 2 tablespoons cornstarch and 1 tablespoon cold water. Add to hot mixture. Cook and stir until thick and bubbly.

Makes about 1 ¾ cups

Gravies and Sauces

WHITE SAUCE

2 tablespoons cornstarch
1/4 teaspoon salt
1 cup soy milk

Blend cornstarch into milk. Cook over medium heat, stirring constantly until thick. Add salt. Continue cooking slowly for 5 minutes. Remove from heat and serve hot over broccoli or cooked pasta.

Makes about 1 cup

BECHAMEL SAUCE

1/4 cup oil
1/3 cup white flour
2 cups water
1/2 cup soy milk powder
4 teaspoons dried chives
1 teaspoon salt

Blend together the water, soy milk powder, chives, and salt. Heat the oil in a saucepan, then lightly brown flour in the oil. Slowly add the water mixture to saucepan mixture, stirring constantly until thick. Continue to cook for 5 minutes. Serve hot.

Makes about 2 1/2 cups

Chapter Five

ONION SAUCE

1 medium onion sliced thinly into rounds
1 ½ tablespoons cornstarch
1 ½ cups water
½ teaspoon salt
¼ teaspoon basil

Saute onions in water over medium heat for 5 minutes. Mix cornstarch with a small amount of water, then add to onions. Stir in salt and basil, then simmer for 15 minutes over low heat.

Makes about 2 cups

TOMATO RELISH

2 medium tomatoes, peeled and finely chopped
1 medium onion, chopped
1 teaspoon salt
¼ teaspoon ground cumin
¼ clove garlic, minced

Mix all ingredients. Cover and refrigerate. Do not keep longer than one week. Serve with enchiladas, tostadas, burritos, or refried beans.

Makes about 2 cups

Gravies and Sauces

SEASONED TOMATO SAUCE

1 tablespoon oil
2 tablespoons chopped onion
2 tablespoons chopped green pepper
1 can (8 ounces) tomato sauce
salt to taste

Heat oil in saucepan. Add onion and green pepper; cook and stir until tender. Stir in tomato sauce and salt. Cook over low heat for 15-20 minutes, stirring occasionally.

Makes about 1 1/4 cups

GARLIC TOMATO SAUCE

3 cloves garlic, minced
1 tablespoon olive oil
1 can (16 ounces) whole tomatoes
1 small onion, chopped
1/2 teaspoon salt
1/4 teaspoon dried basil leaves
1/4 teaspoon dried rosemary leaves, crushed

Cook all ingredients in a saucepan over medium heat until boiling. Break up tomatoes in saucepan with a fork. Reduce heat. Simmer, uncovered, stirring occasionally, until sauce thickens.

Makes about 1 1/2 cups

Chapter Five

SPAGHETTI SAUCE

2 large onions, chopped
4 cloves garlic, crushed
2 teaspoons salt
2 teaspoons dried oregano leaves
2 teaspoons dried basil leaves
1 teaspoon dried marjoram leaves
1 teaspoon Italian seasoning
1 bay leaf
2 tablespoons sugar
2 cans (15 ounces) tomato sauce
1 can (12 ounces) tomato paste
1 can (28 ounces) whole tomatoes

Place chopped canned tomatoes and their juice in large saucepan along with remaining ingredients. Mix well. Add water if thinner sauce is desired. Simmer for 1 hour stirring occasionally.

Serves 4-6

Gravies and Sauces

ITALIAN TOMATO SAUCE

1 teaspoon oil
1/3 cup water
1 cup onions, chopped small
2 teaspoons sweet basil
2 teaspoons sugar
1/2 teaspoon marjoram
1/2 teaspoon oregano
3/4 teaspoons garlic powder
4 cups canned crushed tomatoes
1 teaspoon salt

Saute first three ingredients until onions are tender. Add remaining ingredients, simmer for 30 minutes to blend flavors. Serve hot over pasta.

Serves 4

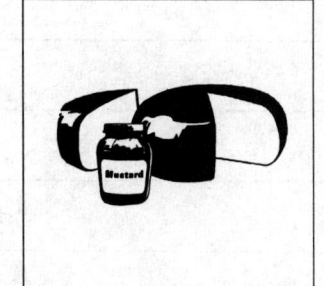

Cheeses, Spreads and Condiments

CHEESES, SPREADS AND CONDIMENTS

Agar Cheese	174
Almond Butter	190
Apple Butter	190
Basic Sauce	186
Cashew Butter	191
Catsup	180
Chee Sauce	178
Cucumber Dip	188
Cucumber Spinach Dip	187
Date Butter	191
Date Nut Spread	191
Dill Mayonnaise	181
Eggplant Dip	188
Golden Garbanzo Dip	187
Guacamole	183
Home Made Chicken Style Seasoning	192
Humus	185
Lemon and Oil Sauce	179

Mayo Spread	182
Mayonnaise	181
Melty Cheez	176
Mock American Cheese	177
Mustard	180
Parsley-Chive Dip	189
Party Spread	183
Pimento Cheese	175
Relish	182
Salsa	179
Sandwich Spread	183
Seasoned Salt	192
Sesame Tahini	185
Sour Cream	184
Tasty Cheese Sauce	176
Tofu Sour Cream	184
Tomato Topping	178

Chapter Six

AGAR CHEESE

¼ cup Agar
1 cup Water
¾ cup Sesame Seed
1 can Pimentos
1 teaspoon salt
1 teaspoon Onion Powder
1 cup Oil
½ cup Lemon Juice

Soak agar in water about 5 minutes, then boil gently until clear. While agar is boiling, place next five ingredients in blender and whirl until smooth. Add the hot agar, whirl ½ minute. Add the lemon juice last, and mix for only a second. Immediately, pour into mold and set in refrigerator to cool. Slice thinly onto a platter. Garnish with parsley. Another way to serve this cheese is to cut it into 1 inch cubes and sprinkle with sesame seed for decoration. For variation, use ¼ cup of food yeast in the recipe or ¾ cup cashews in place of the sesame seed.

Cheeses, Spreads and Condiments

PIMENTO CHEESE

1 cup water
½ cup white flour
⅓ cup oil
⅓ cup yeast flakes
1 teaspoon salt
1 teaspoon onion powder
½ teaspoon garlic powder
7 ounces pimento
1 tablespoon lemon juice

Blend all ingredients in blender until smooth. Put mixture into small baking dish and bake at 350 degrees 40 minutes. Chill.

Chapter Six

MELTY CHEEZ

Blend until smooth:

1/3 cup yeast flakes
1/3 white flour
3 tablespoons cornstarch
2 tablespoons oil
1 1/2 teaspoons salt
2 cups water
1 1/2 teaspoons lemon juice
1/2 cup canned tomatoes

Pour mixture into saucepan and cook over low heat until thick, stirring constantly.

TASTY CHEESE SAUCE

1/2 cup yeast flakes
1/4 cup vegetable oil
1/2 cup tomato pieces
3 tablespoons cornstarch
2 cups water
1 1/2 teaspoons salt
1/3 cup flour
1 tablespoon lemon juice.

Blend all ingredients together in a blender, then cook in a saucepan over medium heat until thick.

Cheeses, Spreads and Condiments

MOCK AMERICAN CHEESE

1 cup water
1/2 cup white flour
1/2 cup yeast flakes
1/2 cup tahini
1 tablespoon onion powder
1/2 teaspoon garlic powder
1/2 cup pimento
1 1/2 teaspoon salt
2 tablespoons lemon juice

Blend all ingredients in blender until smooth. Put mixture into small baking dish and bake at 350 degrees for 20 minutes. Chill well, then cube or slice. You may pour 1/4 inch deep in a large baking pan, bake until done, but only lightly browned. Slice with a pizza cutter into sandwich-size squares.

Chapter Six

CHEE SAUCE

3 cups water
2 ¼ cups cashews
6 tablespoons sesame seeds
4 teaspoons salt
½ cup yeast flakes
1 tablespoon onion powder
½ garlic powder
½ teaspoon dill seed
1 ½ cups pimento
¾ cup lemon juice

Blend all ingredients in blender until smooth. If using as chee sauce for lasagna blend in 2 cups oats.

TOMATO TOPPING

1 cup finely chopped fresh salad tomatoes
¼ teaspoon dried basil, crushed
2 tablespoons oil

Blend tomatoes and basil with oil. Serve on cooked green beans, cauliflower, or lima beans.

Makes about 1 cup

Cheeses, Spreads and Condiments

SALSA

2 1/2 cups chopped onion
1 1/2 cups chopped green pepper
2 1/2 cups tomato juice
1 1/4 cups pineapple juice
1/4 cup lemon juice
1/2 teaspoon sweet basil
1/2 teaspoon cumin
1/2 teaspoon salt
1/2 teaspoon garlic powder
1/3 cup tomato paste

Saute onions and peppers in 1/4 cup water over low heat until tender. Meanwhile heat remaining ingredients and simmer 10 minutes. Mix all ingredients together. Use warm with chips or chill.

Makes about 4 1/2 cups

LEMON AND OIL SAUCE

1/3 cup vegetable oil
1/3 cup lemon juice
1/4 teaspoon salt

Blend until creamy and serve over any salad or steamed vegetables.

Makes about 2/3 cup

Chapter Six

CATSUP

1 cup tomato paste
2 teaspoons corn syrup
1 ½ teaspoons salt
¼ cup lemon juice
¼ teaspoon garlic powder
¼ teaspoon onion powder

Mix all ingredients together until very smooth. Chill.

Makes about 1 ¼ cups

MUSTARD

1 cup water
½ cup flour
2 teaspoons turmeric
1 teaspoon salt
½ teaspoon garlic powder
⅔ cup oil

Blend first 4 ingredients until smooth. Put mixture into small saucepan and cook over medium heat until thick. Return to blender add garlic powder and oil. Blend until smooth. Add 1 cup lemon juice while still blending. Chill.

Makes about 1 ½ cups

Cheeses, Spreads and Condiments

MAYONNAISE

3/4 cup water
1/2 cup soy milk powder
1 1/2 teaspoon onion powder
1 teaspoon salt
1/2 cup oil
1 1/2 teaspoon lemon juice

Blend together all ingredients except oil until smooth. While still blending slowly add oil. Put mixture into bowl and fold in lemon juice. Chill.

Makes about 1 1/2 cups

DILL MAYONNAISE

1 cup MAYONNAISE
1 teaspoon dried dill weed
3 tablespoons lemon juice
dash salt

Mix MAYONNAISE, chives, and salt. Fold in lemon juice. Chill.

Makes about 1 cup

Chapter Six

MAYO SPREAD

5 tablespoons pastry flour (white or whole wheat)
1 cup water
1/2 teaspoon salt
2 tablespoons lemon juice
2 tablespoons vegetable oil

Combine the flour and water in a small saucepan and bring to a boil, whisking constantly. Cook until thick. Cool at room temperature. Place the cooled mixture in a blender along with the salt and half of the lemon juice. Blend on medium speed slowly adding the oil and the rest of the lemon juice. Mix well. Refrigerate.

Makes about 1 1/4 cups

RELISH

1 cup MAYONNAISE
1/4 cup chopped pimentos
1/4 cup minced celery
1/4 cup chopped green onion
1/4 cup chopped parsley
1/4 cup minced peeled cucumber

Mix all ingredients and chill.

Makes about 2 1/4 cups

Cheeses, Spreads and Condiments

SANDWICH SPREAD

1 cup MAYONNAISE
1/2 teaspoon onion powder
Brewers yeast flakes

Mix MAYONNAISE and onion powder together. Add enough flaked food yeast to make a thick spread. Chill.

Makes about 1 cup

GUACAMOLE

Mash 2 peeled and pitted avocados with fork. Stir in 1 tablespoon grated onion, 1 tablespoon lemon juice, 1 teaspoon salt, 1/4 teaspoon cumin. Add 1/3 cup MAYONNAISE. Chill.

PARTY SPREAD

1 cup CHEE SAUCE
1/4 cup sliced black olives
1/3 cup MAYONNAISE
1/4 cup minced onion

Mix thoroughly and chill. Serve with chips or use as a spread on sandwiches.

Makes about 2 cups

Chapter Six

SOUR CREAM

Mix 1 cup MAYONNAISE, 1/4 cup snipped chives, 3 tablespoons lemon juice, and dash of salt. Chill. Delicious over baked potatoes.

Makes about 1 1/4 cups

TOFU SOUR CREAM

---

1 cup tofu, well drained
1 tablespoon fresh lemon juice
1/4 teaspoon salt
1/2 teaspoon nutritional yeast

Place all ingredients in a blender and blend until creamy. Chill.

Makes about 1 cup

Cheeses, Spreads and Condiments

HUMUS

4 cups cooked garbanzos
½ cup lemon juice
2 tablespoons salt
1 cup tahini, or 2 cups sesame seed ground to a powder in a seed mill
2 teaspoons onion powder
1 ½ teaspoons garlic powder
⅔ cup water or garbanzo juice

Blend all ingredients in blender until smooth and creamy. Serve with crackers or fresh vegetables.

Makes about 5 cups

SESAME TAHINI

1 cup sesame butter
⅓ cup corn syrup

Mix together until smooth. Small amount of oil may be needed if butter is dry. Consistency should be smooth and creamy with no lumps. Spread on toast, bread, or drizzle on desserts.

Makes about 1 ⅓ cups

Chapter Six

BASIC SAUCE

2 cups water
1 cup soy milk powder
2 teaspoons salt
2 teaspoons onion powder

Blend all ingredients in blender until well mixed, then add 1 1/2 cups oil slowly. Fold in by hand 3 tablespoons lemon juice. Store refrigerated in a covered container.

For SOUR CREAM add 2 more tablespoons lemon juice.
For DILL DRESSING add 2 teaspoons dill weed.
For THOUSAND ISLAND DRESSING add 2 tablespoons pickle relish and 1 tablespoon finely chopped ripe tomato or pimento.

Cheeses, Spreads and Condiments

GOLDEN GARBANZO DIP

2 cups cooked garbanzos
1 cup canned tomatoes
1 1/2 teaspoons onion powder
1 teaspoon salt
2 tablespoons lemon juice
1/4 cup yeast flakes
1/3 cup tahini
1/4 teaspoon garlic powder

Blend all ingredients in blender until smooth. Chill.

Makes about 3 cups

CUCUMBER SPINACH DIP

1 pound frozen or fresh chopped spinach
1 large cucumber sliced
3 green onions with tops, sliced
1/2 cup MAYONNAISE
1 tablespoon lemon juice
1/2 teaspoon garlic powder
Pinch cumin

Steam the spinach and drain. Place drained spinach and remaining ingredients in a blender and blend until smooth. Chill. Serve with chips, crackers, or raw vegetables.

Makes about 2 cups

Chapter Six

EGGPLANT DIP

1 large eggplant
1 clove garlic, minced
½ teaspoon salt
1 teaspoon lemon juice

Place the eggplant on a baking dish, poke several holes in the top for steam to escape. Bake for one hour in oven at 350 degrees. Cut off the stem greens and cut the eggplant in half lengthwise. Remove the skin and discard. Put pulp into the baking dish, removing seeds if they are large. Cut the pulp into chunks and return to the oven at 350 degrees for 15 minutes. Cool for 15 minutes. Put pulp in blender with garlic, salt, and lemon juice. Puree until mixture is smooth. Serve with crackers or chips.

CUCUMBER DIP

Cut medium peeled cucumber in half lengthwise. Remove seeds. Shred enough cucumber to make 1 cup. Don't drain. Combine with 3 cups SOUR CREAM, 1 tablespoon parsley, 2 tablespoons minced onion, 2 teaspoons lemon juice, ¼ teaspoon salt. Mix well. Chill.

Makes about 4 cups

Cheeses, Spreads and Condiments

PARSLEY-CHIVE DIP

5 tablespoons flour
1 cup soy milk
1 tablespoon olive oil
2 tablespoons lemon juice
2 tablespoons fresh parsley
2 tablespoons chopped chives

Combine flour and soy milk in small saucepan. Bring to a boil, stirring constantly, and cook until thick. Remove from heat and chill for 30 minutes. After chilled, put mixture in a blender with lemon juice and blend. While still blending add oil, parsley, and chives. Chill for 30 minutes before serving. Use for vegetable sticks, crackers, bread sticks, or salad topping.

Chapter Six

ALMOND BUTTER

2 cups blanched almonds
1 tablespoon oil
Salt to taste

Place almonds in grinder and blend to the desired consistency. Remove nuts from grinder and place in a bowl. Add oil and salt, mix well.

Makes about 1 ½ cups

APPLE BUTTER

1 quart applesauce
2 teaspoons vanilla
1 teaspoon coriander

Mix ingredients well. Place in casserole dish 1 inch deep. Bake at 150 degrees overnight. Can be served warm or chilled.

DATE BUTTER

5 cups chopped dates
3 cups hot water
2 teaspoons orange rind, unsprayed

Soak dates in hot water until soft. Blend until smooth with orange rind.

DATE NUT SPREAD

Make half of DATE BUTTER recipe. Add 1 ½ cups finely chopped walnuts.

CASHEW BUTTER

2 cups raw cashew pieces
2 ½ teaspoons vegetable oil

Place the cashews in a blender and grind them into a meal at medium speed. Add the oil and blend until creamy, about 5 minutes. Salt can be added if desired.

Chapter Six

SEASONED SALT

½ cup salt
1 tablespoon celery salt
1 tablespoon garlic salt
1 tablespoon paprika
1 teaspoon onion powder

Mix all ingredients together. Store in a tightly covered container.

HOME MADE CHICKEN STYLE SEASONING

½ cup food yeast
2 ½ teaspoons sweet pepper flakes (powdered)
3 teaspoons onion powder
3 ½ teaspoons salt
2 ½ teaspoons sage
2 ½ teaspoons thyme
2 ½ teaspoons garlic powder
2 ¼ teaspoons marjoram
1 ¼ teaspoons rosemary

Mix all ingredients. Store in a tightly closed container.
May be used in place of McKay's Chicken Style seasoning if desired.

Cheeses, Spreads and Condiments

Notes

Vegetables

VEGETABLES

Baked Stuffed Tomatoes	207
Braised Cabbage	203
Broccoli with Chee Sauce	209
Carrots Piquant	210
Cauliflower Medley	208
Chived Carrots	211
Corn and Onions	212
Corn Pot Pie	213
Country Limas	205
Creamed Carrots	210
Creamed Vegetables	211
Creole Green Beans	206
French Fries	216
Glazed Beets	215
Green Beans and Tomatoes	206

Harvard Beets	214
Italian Broccoli	209
Italian Corn	212
Mashed Potato Bake	216
Oriental Cabbage	203
Oven Peas	213
Peppered Zucchini	204
Potato Croquettes	217
Saucy Cauliflower	208
Savory Broccoli	209
Scalloped Eggplant	204
Scalloped Potatoes	218
Spinach Potatoes	219
Sweet Potato Croquettes	217
Sweet Potato Bake	219

Chapter Seven

COOKING VEGETABLES

ARTICHOKES: Wash, trim stems, and remove lose outer leaves. Cut sharp leave tips off. In a large covered cooking pot simmer in 3 inches of boiling salted water until a leaf pulls off easily, 20-30 minutes.

ASPARAGUS: Wash and scrape off scales. Break off woody base. Leave spears whole. Prop tips up out of water onto crumpled foil. Cook, covered, in a small amount of boiling salted water 10-15 minutes.

BEANS, GREEN: Wash, then remove ends and strings. Leave whole or cut into pieces. Cook, covered, in a small amount of boiling salted water 20-30 minutes.

BEETS: Cut off all but 1 inch of stems and roots. Do not peel beets. Cook, covered, in boiling salted water until tender, 30-45 minutes. Cool slightly, then slip off skins.

BROCCOLI: Remove outer leaves and tough parts of stalk, then wash. Cut lengthwise into spears. Cook, covered, in 1-2 inches of boiling salted water until desired tenderness, 5-10 minutes.

BRUSSELS SPROUTS: Trim stems, remove wilted leaves, then wash. Cook, covered, in 2 inches of boiling salted water until tender, about 10-15 minutes.

Vegetables

CABBAGE: Remove wilted outer leaves, then wash. Cut into wedges, remove center core. Cook, uncovered, in a small amount of boiling salted water for 5 minutes, then cover and continue to cook 5-10 minutes longer.

CARROTS: Wash, trim, and peel. Slice, dice, or cut into sticks. Cook, covered, in 2 inches of boiling salted water 10-20 minutes.

CAULIFLOWER: Remove leaves and woody stems. Wash, then break into flowerets. Cook, covered, in a small amount of boiling salted water 10-15 minutes.

CORN: For cut corn, cut off the tips of kernels. Scrape cobs with dull edge of a knife. Cook, covered, in a small amount of boiling salted water 12-15 minutes. For corn on the cob, cook, covered, in a small amount of boiling salted water for 8-10 minutes. Or for baked corn on the cob, wrap each ear in foil. Bake in oven at 450 degrees about 30 minutes, turning several times during baking.

EGGPLANT: Wash then cut off cap. Cut crosswise into $\frac{1}{2}$-inch thick slices. Saute on both sides in hot vegetable oil, 2 minutes per side.

GREENS: Thoroughly wash in cool water. Cut off roots, remove damaged leaves and large veins. Cook, covered, in boiling salted water until just tender. Cooking time will vary depending on type. About 15-60 minutes.

Chapter Seven

OKRA: Wash pods then cut off stems. Cook, covered, in a small amount of boiling salted water 10-15 minutes.

PEAS, GREEN: Shell and wash. Cook, covered, in a small amount of boiling salted water until tender, 10 minutes.

POTATOES: Scrub thoroughly, remove green areas. Cook with skins on, or peel, and quarter or cube. Cook, covered in boiling salted water 25-40 minutes for whole potatoes, 20-25 minutes for quartered potatoes, or 10-15 minutes for tiny new potatoes. For baked potatoes, scrub then prick with a fork. Wrap in foil if desired, then bake in oven at 350 degrees for 1 $\frac{1}{2}$ hours or until tender through to the middle. Turn potatoes one time during cooking, about half way through cooking time.

SWEET POTATOES: Scrub, then cut off woody portions and ends. Peel or cook in skins, depending on use. Cook, covered, in enough boiling salted water to cover 25-30 minutes, or bake whole in oven at 375 degrees 40-45 minutes.

RUTABAGAS: Wash, peel, then slice or cube. Cook in 2 inches of boiling salted water, 25-30 minutes.

SPINACH: Wash thoroughly in lukewarm water. Cook, covered in a very small amount of water. Reduce heat when steam begins. Turn often with a fork. Cook 3-5 minutes after steam begins.

Vegetables

SQUASH, WINTER: Wash, cut in half, then remove seeds and strings. Place cut side down in a baking pan. Cover and bake in oven at 350 degrees for 30 minutes. Turn cut side up and continue to bake covered for 20 to 30 minutes longer. Hubbard or banana squash need to continue baking 45-50 minutes.

SQUASH, SUMMER: Wash, cut off ends, then slice. Cook in a small amount of boiling salted water, 5-10 minutes.

TOMATOES: Wash, remove stems and core, then peel. Cut up or cook whole. In a covered pan cook slowly without added water, 10-15 minutes.

TURNIPS: Wash and peel, then slice or cube. Cook in 2 inches of boiling salted water, 15-20 minutes.

ZUCCHINI: Wash, cut off ends, then slice. Cook in a small amount of boiling salted water, 5-10 minutes.

RAW FRUITS AND VEGETABLES

To get a sufficient supply of vitamin C and to properly exercise the teeth and jaws, some food should be eaten raw at every meal. Most fruits and vegetables can be eaten raw. An abundant supply of raw fruits and vegetables should be provided, at least one dish at each meal.

Chapter Seven

VEGETABLES

As one of the essential four food groups, vegetables furnish a major portion of vitamins, proteins, and minerals. Most vegetables have oils and carbohydrates in varying quantities. The other three essential food groups are fruits, nuts, and grains. These four together furnish all the nutrients we need for development of growth, maintenance of health, and recovery from illness.

Use as many vegetables in season as can be obtained. Handle vegetables promptly after picking to avoid the loss of nutrients that comes from long delays in processing, standing in sunshine, wilting, or softening. Paring, shredding, and slicing should be done immediately before use or processing to avoid nutrient losses. Vitamin C is especially vulnerable to loss.

Fresh succulent vegetables should be cooked as little as possible. Over cooking toughens the texture of some vegetable foods, destroys the coloring, and damages the minerals that contribute to their flavor and nutritive value. Vegetables should be allowed to boil slowly. Rapid boiling hardens some foods. Steaming of vegetables hastens the cooking, shortens the time of meal preparation, and preserves the nutrients best. Use only sufficient water to produce the steam needed.

BRAISED CABBAGE

1 large head of cabbage
1 cup water
2 cloves of garlic, minced
1 teaspoon salt

Shred cabbage into desired size and place in cooking pot with water, garlic, and salt. Steam cabbage to desired tenderness.

Serves 4-6

ORIENTAL CABBAGE

1 small head green cabbage
2 tablespoons vegetable oil
2 medium celery stalks, sliced thin
1 medium green pepper, cut into thin slices
1 large onion, chopped
1 teaspoon salt

Wash cabbage and remove outer leaves. Cut into thin wedges. Heat oil in a skillet. Stir in cabbage, celery, green pepper, and onion. Cover and cook over medium heat, stirring occasionally, until vegetables are tender.

Serves 4-6

Chapter Seven

PEPPERED ZUCCHINI

1 pound zucchini
1 onion, thinly sliced
1 small green pepper, chopped
2 tablespoons vegetable oil
1 teaspoon salt
2 tomatoes, cut into wedges

Cut zucchini into 1/4-inch slices. Saute zucchini, onion, and green pepper, in oil, until tender. Add salt and tomatoes; cook over low heat until tomatoes are hot. Sprinkle with snipped parsley.

Serves 4

SCALLOPED EGGPLANT

8 cups eggplant, cubed and steamed
2 cups bread crumbs
1 teaspoon salt
2-3 cups BECHAMEL SAUCE, medium consistency

Mix and place in a casserole dish, top with bread crumbs. Bake at 350 degrees for 45 minutes.

Serves 4-6

COUNTRY LIMAS

1 cup dried lima beans
1 medium onion, cut into ¼ inch slices
½ cup tomato juice
2 tablespoons light molasses
1 tablespoon packed brown sugar
1 tablespoon cumin
1 teaspoon salt
2 tablespoons imitation bacon pieces

Heat beans and add enough water to cover; boil 2 minutes. Remove from heat; cover and let stand 1 hour. Add enough water to beans to cover if necessary. Heat to boiling; reduce heat. Simmer uncovered until tender. Drain beans, reserving liquid. Layer beans and onion in ungreased casserole dish. Mix tomato juice, molasses, brown sugar, cumin, and salt; pour over beans. Add enough reserved bean liquid to cover. Cover and cook in oven at 300 degrees for 1 hour. Stir in imitation bacon pieces.

Serves 4-6

Chapter Seven

GREEN BEANS AND TOMATOES

4 cups cooked green beans
4 tablespoons oil
1/2 cup onion, chopped
1/4 cup green pepper, diced
1 cup canned tomatoes
1 teaspoon flour
1 teaspoon salt

Saute green beans, onion, and green pepper in oil until lightly browned. Mix flour and salt with tomatoes. Add to green bean mixture and cook slowly for 8 to 10 minutes.

Serves 4

CREOLE GREEN BEANS

Cook 1/2 cup chopped onion and 2 cloves crushed garlic in 2 tablespoons of oil until tender. Add 1/4 cup tomato sauce, 1/8 teaspoon salt, and 1 pound cooked fresh green beans, drained. Heat, stirring often.

Serves 4

BAKED STUFFED TOMATOES

6 medium tomatoes
1 green pepper, finely chopped
1 ½ cups COUNTRY BREAD STUFFING
1 teaspoon salt

Remove stem ends from tomatoes; cut thin slice from bottom of each tomato to prevent tipping. Remove pulp from each tomato, leaving a ½-inch wall; chop enough pulp to measure ⅓ cup. Mix tomato pulp, green pepper, stuffing and salt. Fill tomatoes with stuffing mixture. Place filled tomatoes in ungreased baking dish. Cook uncovered in oven at 350 degrees until tomatoes are heated through.

Serves 6

Chapter Seven

SAUCY CAULIFLOWER

1 head cauliflower
salt to taste
2 cups chopped tomatoes
2 tablespoons flour
2 tablespoons water

Break cauliflower head into pieces and cook with salt until tender. Drain well and place in oiled casserole dish. Put tomatoes in saucepan and bring to a boil. Make a paste of flour and water and add to tomatoes. Cook until thickened. Add more water if thinner sauce is desired. Pour sauce over cauliflower. Top with bread crumbs if desired. Bake in oven at 375 degrees for 20 to 30 minutes.

Serves 4

CAULIFLOWER MEDLEY

3 tablespoons oil
2 cups small fresh cauliflower, use just the flowering tops
2-10 ounce packages frozen peas
1 teaspoon salt
2 tablespoons chopped pimento

Heat oil in skillet. Add cauliflower and cook covered over low heat for 10 minutes. Stir occasionally. Add peas and salt. Cook covered 5-10 minutes longer. Stir in pimento.

Serves 4

ITALIAN BROCCOLI

Steam 1½ pounds fresh broccoli in salted water until tender. Drain, then return to cooking pot. Add 3 tablespoons olive oil and 1 teaspoon Italian seasoning, and cook over medium heat until broccoli is lightly browned.

Serves 4

BROCCOLI WITH CHEE SAUCE

1½ pounds fresh broccoli
1 cup CHEE SAUCE

Steam broccoli in boiling salted water until tender. Drain. Cover with heated CHEE SAUCE. Serve immediately.

Serves 4

SAVORY BROCCOLI

Cut 1 head of broccoli, into pieces, steam, then drain. Stir in 2 tablespoons of oil and 1 teaspoon dried dill weed. Serve immediately.

Serves 4

Chapter Seven

CREAMED CARROTS

4 cups carrots, sliced
salt to taste
3 tablespoons oil
1 small onion, minced
3 tablespoons flour
1 ½ cups soy milk

Cook carrots in boiling salt water until tender, then drain. Place in oiled casserole dish. Heat oil. Add onion and cook until tender. Add flour and stir until smooth. Gradually add milk, stirring constantly, and cook until thickened. Pour sauce over carrots and stir gently. Bake in oven at 350 degrees for 20 minutes.

Serves 4

CARROTS PIQUANT

Drain 2 pounds canned small whole carrots reserving ¼ cup of liquid. In saucepan blend 1 tablespoon cornstarch with ¼ teaspoon salt and 1 teaspoon coriander. Stir the carrot liquid and ⅔ cup lemon juice into above mixture. Cook over medium heat stirring constantly until thick and bubbly. Boil 2 minutes longer stirring constantly. Add carrots and continue to cook until carrots are hot.

Serves 4

CHIVED CARROTS

1 ½ pounds fresh carrots
1 tablespoons oil
¼ teaspoon salt
1 tablespoon snipped chives

Peel and slice carrots, then steam in boiling salted water. Drain. Heat oil in skillet, add carrots. Sprinkle with salt and chives. Heat, turning occasionally to coat with oil, until carrots are hot.

Serves 4

CREAMED VEGETABLES

1 tablespoon oil
1 tablespoon flour
¾ cup soy milk
2 cups hot cooked vegetables (any single vegetable or combination)

Heat oil, blend in flour and dash salt. Add milk all at once. Cook quickly stirring constantly until thick. Pour over vegetables.

Serves 2-4

Chapter Seven

CORN AND ONIONS

Heat 2 tablespoons oil in skillet. Add ½ cup chopped onion, season with salt. Cook over low heat 4 minutes stirring occasionally. Add 12 ounces whole kernel corn, drained. Add 1 teaspoon dried basil. Mix. Cook over medium heat for 5 minutes.

Serves 4

ITALIAN CORN

2 - 17 ounce cans whole kernel corn, undrained
1 small onion, chopped
2 cloves garlic, crushed
1 teaspoon basil
1 teaspoon savory

Place all ingredients in cooking pot. Bring to a boil, cook over medium heat until onions are tender.

Serves 4-6

Vegetables

CORN POT PIE

Pastry for double crust pie
3 cups fresh corn
2 cups raw potatoes, diced
Salt to taste
3 tablespoons flour
1 1/2 cups soy milk

Line a casserole dish with pastry. Combine corn, potatoes, and salt, then pour into pastry lined casserole dish. Mix flour and soy milk until smooth. Pour over corn and potatoes. Cover with top pastry. Pinch edges to seal, and cut several slits in top crust for ventilation. Bake in oven at 425 degrees for 35 minutes.

Serves 4-6

OVEN PEAS

In a 1 1/2 quart casserole dish combine 2 - 10 ounce packages frozen peas, thawed enough to separate, 1 cup minced onion, 1 teaspoon salt, 1/2 teaspoon dried savory, 1 tablespoon oil, and 1/4 cup water. Cover and bake at 350 degrees for 1 hour.

Serves 6

Chapter Seven

HARVARD BEETS

5 fresh medium beets
1 tablespoon cornstarch
1 tablespoon sugar
¾ teaspoon salt
⅔ cup water
¼ cup lemon juice

Cut off all but 2 inches of beet tops. Wash beets and leave whole with root ends attached. Heat 6 cups water, 1 teaspoon lemon juice and 1 teaspoon salt to boiling. Add beets. Cover and boil gently until tender, 35 to 40 minutes. Drain. Run cold water over beets; slip off skins and remove root ends. Cut into slices. Mix cornstarch, sugar, and salt in saucepan. Stir water and lemon juice gradually into cornstarch mixture. Cook, stirring constantly, until mixture thickens and boils. Boil and stir 1 minute. Stir in beets; heat through.

If using canned beets, use 1 can (16 ounces), drained (reserve liquid). Add enough water to reserved liquid to measure ⅔ cup; substitute for water.

Serves 4

Vegetables

GLAZED BEETS

1 pound cooked sliced beets
1 tablespoon cornstarch
½ teaspoon salt
3 tablespoons firmly packed brown sugar
1 cup orange juice

Drain beets. In saucepan combine cornstarch, salt, and brown sugar. Gradually add orange juice. Cook stirring constantly until thick. Add beets. Heat.

Serves 4

Chapter Seven

MASHED POTATO BAKE

2 tablespoons oil
1/2 cup celery, chopped
1/2 cup onion, chopped
4 cups soft bread cubes
1/2 cup boiling water
2 cups soy milk
1 1/2 teaspoon salt
2 cups mashed potatoes

Heat oil. Add celery and onion. Cook until tender. Pour over bread cubes and mix well. Add boiling water to bread and mix. Add remaining ingredients to bread, mixing well. Mixture will be very moist. Turn into oiled casserole dish. Bake at 350 degrees for 45 minutes.

Serves 2-4

FRENCH FRIES

4 large potatoes
2 tablespoons oil

Potatoes may be used peeled, or unpeeled. Cut potatoes into strips 1/2" wide. Dry thoroughly on towel. Place in a bowl, sprinkle with salt, and drizzle with the oil. Toss lightly to distribute oil evenly. Spread french fries evenly in a single layer on a cookie sheet. Cook in preheated oven, at 375 degrees, for 25 minutes turning when half done. Turn on broiler for last 1-2 minutes to complete the browning.

Serves 4

POTATO CROQUETTES

4 cups mashed potatoes
1/3 cup fresh parsley, chopped
1 cup onion, minced
1 cup grated carrots
1/8 cup soy milk powder
1/8 cup oil
1 1/4 teaspoon salt
2 cloves garlic, crushed

Mix all ingredients well. Form croquettes with ice cream scoop. Place on oiled cookie sheet and bake at 350 degrees for 30-45 minutes, turning after 15 minutes.

Serves 4

SWEET POTATO CROQUETTES

Sweet potatoes
Bread crumbs
Oil

Wash potatoes and cook until tender. Peel potatoes while hot. Mash them immediately, beating until smooth. Chill mashed potatoes for several hours in refrigerator. Shape potatoes into uniform croquettes. Roll in bread crumbs. Fry croquettes in oil, turning so all sides brown, or bake in oven at 350 degrees for about 30 minutes, turning after 15 minutes.

Chapter Seven

SCALLOPED POTATOES

3 tablespoons oil
3 tablespoons white flour
1 ½ teaspoons salt
2 cups soy milk
6 medium potatoes, peeled and sliced
1 small onion chopped
¼ teaspoon oregano
½ teaspoon celery salt
2 cloves of garlic, crushed
1 teaspoon McKay's beef seasoning (optional)

Heat oil in medium saucepan. Add flour stirring constantly to keep from scorching. Add soy milk and salt and cook until bubbly, stirring constantly. Cook 3 minutes over medium heat. Remove from heat. Place the potatoes in oiled 2 quart casserole dish. Pour the sauce over potatoes and mix. Add onions and crushed garlic. Cover and bake in oven at 350 degrees for 1 hour. Uncover and continue to bake for 30 minutes longer.

Serves 4

SWEET POTATO BAKE

6 medium sweet potatoes
1 teaspoon salt
½ cup orange juice
1 can (8 ounces) crushed pineapple, drained

Heat oven to 375 degrees. Pierce sweet potatoes with fork; bake for 45 to 60 minutes or until soft. Remove skins and discard. Place sweet potatoes in a large bowl and mash. Stir in remaining ingredients. Place mixture in a baking dish. Bake in oven at 375 degrees for 15 minutes or until hot.

Serves 4-6

SPINACH POTATOES

10 ounces frozen spinach
8 large potatoes, cooked and mashed
¾ cup SOUR CREAM
2 teaspoons salt
¼ teaspoon cumin
2 teaspoons chopped chives
¼ teaspoon dill weed

Thaw and drain spinach. Combine all ingredients and mix well. Place in an oiled casserole dish and bake in oven at 400 degrees for 20 minutes.

Serves 4-6

Soups

SOUPS

Barley Soup	224
Black Bean Soup	227
Celery Chowder	238
Chicken Noodle Soup	236
Cream of Tomato Soup	233
Elegant Potato Soup	230
French Onion Soup	230
Gazpacho	231
Lentil Parsnip Soup	226
Macaroni Soup	232
Meaty Rice Soup	232
Minestrone	234
Navy Bean Soup	224
Northern Bean Soup	225
Oriental Soup	229

Potato Corn Chowder	237
Split Pea Soup	228
Vegetable Broth	238
Vegetable Cream Soup	233
Vegetable Soup	235
Vegetable Stock	239

Chapter Eight

NAVY BEAN SOUP

7 cups water
1 pound dried navy beans (about 2 cups)
2 medium onions, finely chopped
4 cloves garlic, crushed
1/3 cup fresh parsley, chopped
1/2 teaspoon salt
1 bay leaf

Heat water and beans to boiling in a large cooking pot; boil 2 minutes. Remove from heat; cover and let stand 1 hour. Stir in remaining ingredients. Heat to boiling; reduce heat. Cover and simmer, skimming off foam occasionally, until beans are tender. Do not boil or beans will burst. Add more water during cooking if needed.

Serves 6

BARLEY SOUP

1/4 cup whole barley
1 1/2 cups carrots, sliced
1/2 cup onions, chopped
1 cup celery, sliced
2 cups tomatoes

Cook barley one hour in 6 cups water. Add remaining ingredients and simmer until tender.

Serves 2-4

NORTHERN BEAN SOUP

8 cups water
1 pound dried Great Northern beans (about 2 cups)
1 large onion, chopped
2 tablespoons soy sauce
1 can (8 ounces) tomato sauce
1 teaspoon salt
2 cloves garlic, crushed
2 cups mashed potatoes
2 medium carrots, sliced thin
2 medium stalks celery, sliced thin

Heat water and beans to boiling in a large cooking pot; boil 2 minutes. Remove from heat; cover and let stand 1 hour. Add tomato sauce, onion, soy sauce, salt, and garlic to beans. Heat to boiling, then reduce heat, cover and simmer until beans are nearly done. Do not boil. Stir potatoes, carrots, and celery into soup. Heat to boiling; reduce heat. Cover and simmer until vegetables are tender, about 45 minutes. Stir in more water for thinner consistency if desired.

Serves 4-6

Chapter Eight

LENTIL PARSNIP SOUP

6 cups water
1 cup lentils
3 tablespoons soy sauce
1 bay leaf
1 teaspoon olive oil
1 onion, chopped
2 cloves garlic, chopped
1 celery stalk, sliced thin
1 parsnip, diced
2 carrots, dices
2 tablespoons chopped parsley

In a large soup pot place the water, lentils, soy sauce, and bay leaf. Bring to a boil, reduce heat to medium and cook for 1 1/2 hours. In the meantime, heat the oil in a large skillet. Saute the onions until golden brown. Add the leek, garlic, celery, parsnip, carrots, and parsley. Mix well, cover, and cook for 5 minutes. Add the skillet mixture to the lentils and cook for 30 minutes. Add 1/2 to 1 cup of boiling water to the soup if it becomes to thick.

Serves 2-4

BLACK BEAN SOUP

2 cups black beans
2 onions, chopped
2 carrots, peeled and sliced
1 stalk celery, sliced
2 teaspoons salt
3 quarts water
2 teaspoons basil

Soak the beans overnight in cold water. Drain, then cover beans with fresh water. Bring to a boil with the cold water. Skim off foam, then add remaining ingredients. Cover and simmer 2-4 hours, adding more water if needed. Add more salt if needed.

Serves 4

Chapter Eight

SPLIT PEA SOUP

1 pound dry green split peas
3 teaspoons olive oil
3 cloves garlic, minced
1 large onion, chopped
4 celery stalks, sliced
3 carrots, sliced
2 teaspoons salt
1/8 teaspoon thyme
1/2 teaspoon dried basil

Clean the split peas and let them stand overnight in 2 1/2 quarts of water. Heat the olive oil in a large skillet. Add the garlic, onion, celery, and carrot, and saute over medium heat for 10 minutes. Add the sauteed vegetables, salt, and thyme to the split peas, bring to a boil, and simmer for 2 hours. As foam appears, skim it off and discard. Add more water during cooking if needed. Serve with CROUTONS.

Serves 4

ORIENTAL SOUP

6 cups water
4 scallions, thinly sliced
1 cup bean sprouts
2 cups snow peas, strings removed
1 can bamboo shoots
1 can sliced water chestnuts
1/4 cup soy sauce

Bring the water to a boil. Add the scallions and simmer, covered, for 20 minutes. Add bean sprouts, snow peas, bamboo shoots, water chestnuts, and soy sauce to the broth and cook 10 minutes. Serve at once.

Serves 4

Chapter Eight

ELEGANT POTATO SOUP

6 medium potatoes, peeled
1 cup fresh or canned tomatoes, cut into chunks
2 carrots, peeled and sliced thin
1 tablespoon chopped fresh basil
1 cup VEGETABLE STOCK
Salt to taste

Dice the potatoes. Place in a saucepan covered with water and cook until tender but not mushy. Place two-thirds of the potatoes in a blender and blend until very smooth. Return the potatoes to the saucepan and add remaining ingredients. Bring to a boil and simmer, covered, until the carrots are just tender.

Serves 4-6

FRENCH ONION SOUP

3 medium onions, sliced
2 tablespoons oil
4 cups VEGETABLE STOCK
2 teaspoons soy sauce

Cover and cook onions in oil in 3-quart saucepan over low heat, stirring often, 30 minutes. Add VEGETABLE STOCK and soy sauce; heat to boiling. Reduce heat; cover and simmer 30 minutes. If desired, place ½ slice toasted bread in each of 4 soup bowls; pour hot soup over toast.

Serves 2-4

GAZPACHO

1 large bell pepper
1/2 large onion
1 large carrot, peeled
3 cucumbers, peeled and seeded
2 cloves garlic

Chop all vegetables very fine and add:

1 quart whole tomatoes, chopped
4 3/4 cups tomato juice
3 tablespoons olive oil
1/2 cup lemon juice
1/2 teaspoon oregano

Serve chilled. Flavor gets better the longer it sets.

Chapter Eight

MACARONI SOUP

1 large carrot
2 cups water
2 large onions
1 quart diced potatoes
½ cup uncooked macaroni
1 teaspoon salt
2 cups soy milk

Chop carrot and cook in 2 cups water. While cooking chop onions. When carrot is partially cooked add onions, potatoes, macaroni, and salt. Add enough water to cover and cook until tender. Add milk and heat.

Serves 4

MEATY RICE SOUP

2 cups VEGETARIAN STEAKS, chopped into bite size pieces
2 quarts water, or VEGETABLE BROTH
1 onion, chopped
¾ cup celery, chopped
1 ½ teaspoon salt
1 cup rice, cooked

In a large kettle combine vegetable broth, VEGETARIAN STEAKS, water, onion, celery, and salt. Cook over medium heat for 1 hour. Add rice to kettle and heat.

Serves 4

CREAM OF TOMATO SOUP

Blend until smooth:

1 cup cashews
3 cups water
1 tablespoon onion powder
½ teaspoon salt
2 tablespoons cornstarch
¼ teaspoon oregano

When smooth add 1 quart whole peeled tomatoes and continue to blend for 1 minute longer. Place mixture in a cooking put and bring to a boil. Then immediately reduce heat to medium-low, and cook slowly for 15 minutes. Add salt if needed. Thicken to desired consistency with cornstarch.

Serves 4

VEGETABLE CREAM SOUP

4 cups fresh vegetables (such as peas, broccoli, corn, cauliflower, carrots, potatoes)
4 cups water
4 teaspoons soy sauce

Place all the ingredients in a blender and blend until creamy. Bring to a boil and cook for 5 minutes.

Serves 2-4

Chapter Eight

MINESTRONE

2 teaspoons onion powder
3 cloves garlic, crushed
3 teaspoons salt
½ teaspoon dried marjoram leaves
½ teaspoon dried thyme leaves
1 teaspoon oregano
1 bay leaf
2 teaspoons dried basil
4 medium carrots, sliced
2 large stalks celery, sliced
2 medium onions, chopped
6 medium potatoes, chopped
½ pound fresh green beans, snip ends
1 can (28 ounces) whole tomatoes (cut into pieces, and put into soup with all liquid)
1 - 15 ounce can tomato sauce
16 ounces cut Ziti (pasta)

Place all ingredients, except pasta, in a large cooking pot. Cover with water. Let set for 1 to 2 hours to allow flavors to blend. Bring to a boil; reduce heat. Cover and simmer slowly until carrots are almost tender, about 40 minutes. Add uncooked pasta, turn heat up a little and continue to cook until pasta is done, stirring often. Do not overcook.

Serves 6-8

VEGETABLE SOUP

3 large potatoes, cubed
3 large carrots, sliced
½ pound winter squash, peeled, seeds removed, and cubed
1 cup green onions, sliced
1 ½ cups canned green beans
½ cup canned peas
1 teaspoon salt

Place potatoes, carrots, and squash in a large kettle, add water to cover, and bring to a boil. Turn down heat and simmer for 30 minutes. Remove half of the contents of the pot, mash thoroughly in the blender. Return blended mixture to pot. Add green beans, peas, and onions. Heat and serve warm with CRACKERS.

Serves 4-6

Chapter Eight

CHICKEN NOODLE SOUP

2 cups VEGETARIAN STEAKS, sliced into thin strips
4 medium carrots, cut into 1/2 inch slices
4 medium stalks celery, cut into 1/2 inch slices
1 tablespoon salt
1 teaspoon basil
1 teaspoon celery seed
1 teaspoon garlic powder
1 tablespoon onion powder
1/4 cup soy sauce
2 cups curly pasta, uncooked

Place all ingredients except pasta in large cooking pot, cover with water and bring to a boil. Reduce heat, cover and simmer until carrots are tender. In the meantime cook pasta in boiling salted water until tender. Drain, then add to cooked vegetables and their broth.

Serves 4-6

POTATO CORN CHOWDER

4 cups canned corn
8 medium potatoes, peeled, cubed and boiled until tender
2 ½ cups soy milk
2 medium onions, chopped and sauteed
2 stalks celery, sliced and sauteed
1 teaspoon onion powder
1 teaspoon garlic powder
Salt to taste

Blend in a blender half of the corn and half of the cooked potatoes until creamy. Add a small amount of water if needed for blender to move vegetables around. Pour mixture into a large cooking pot. Add remaining corn, potatoes, onions, celery, onion powder, garlic powder, salt, and desired amount of soy milk (amount will be determined by desired consistency). Cover and simmer over medium-low heat for 30 minutes, stirring often to prevent scorching.

Serves 4-6

Chapter Eight

CELERY CHOWDER

1 large onion, diced
1 tablespoon oil
3 cups green celery, chopped
1 cup potatoes, diced
4 cups soy milk
Salt to taste

Saute onion in oil until soft. Add celery and potatoes. Cover with water and cook until soft. Add soy milk and heat. Add salt.

Serves 2-4

VEGETABLE BROTH

2 cups sliced potatoes, with skins left on
2 cups thinly sliced carrots
2 cups thinly sliced turnips
1 medium onion, chopped
1 cup celery, sliced

Wash the vegetables. Slice and put into a large saucepan. Cover with water. Bring to a boil, and let simmer 2 hours. Strain vegetables from broth. Add salt to taste.

VEGETABLE STOCK

2 onions, chopped
4 carrots, sliced
3 celery stalks, sliced
3 cloves garlic, chopped
3 large tomatoes, chopped
2 small potatoes, unpeeled and chopped
1 teaspoon each, oregano, thyme, basil, bay leaf, and salt

Place all ingredients in a pot and cover with water. Simmer covered for about 1 ½ hours. Strain out the vegetables and discard them. If broth is to bland, add more seasonings and cook for 15 minutes longer before straining.

Salads

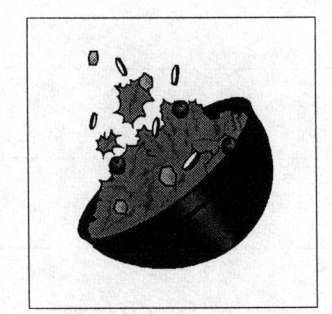

SALADS

Ambrosia	257
Apple Salad	257
Avocado Bowl	252
Broccoli Salad	249
Coleslaw	250
Cucumber Onion Salad	249
Delicious Golden Fruit Dish	256
Garden Stuffed Tomatoes	251
Hawaiian Coleslaw	251
Hot 5 Bean Salad	248
Hot Potato Salad	254
Macaroni Salad	252
Mandrin Citrus Coconut Bowl	255
Potato Salad	253

Spinach Salad	247
Taco Salad	255
Three Bean Salad	247
Tossed Salad	246
Vegetable Salad	246
Waldorf Salad	256
Zucchini Toss	250

Chapter Nine

SALADS

The most familiar salad is the tossed green salad. You can introduce interesting tastes and textures by combining a variety of salad greens. Besides the basic salad greens; Iceberg Lettuce, Leaf Lettuce, Bibb Lettuce, Romaine, and Spinach to name a few, Swiss chard, mustard greens, beet tops, kale leaves, and dandelion greens make good additions to mixed green salads. Use full-flavored greens in small amounts.

Vegetable salads can be either appetizers, side dishes, or main dishes. Fruit salads can be served the same. Either salad can be tossed, layered, or arranged any way you please.

POTATO SALAD TIPS

Boil potatoes in their skins, then drain. Peel potatoes while still warm, then slice or cube the potatoes. To prevent sticking, toss lightly with a few tablespoons of vegetable oil if desired. Cover and chill until ready to use.

SPROUTS

In winter, when greens are in short supply and are expensive, sprouts can be prepared in your own kitchen at a very low price. Sprouts can be used separately with a little salad dressing, or used with other greens, tomatoes, celery, bell pepper, etc., as a tossed salad.

Any seed that will grow can be sprouted in a jar, and used for food. A favorite is alfalfa. It is quite nutritious, being high in calcium and containing also the minerals magnesium, aluminum, sodium, potassium, sulphur, silicon, chlorine, and phosphorus. Alfalfa seed contain the entire B complex and are a good source of vitamins A, C, D, and E.

SALAD TOPPINGS

Top salads with 1 of the following: CROUTONS, toasted pumpkin seeds, peanuts, broken pecans or walnuts, imitation bacon pieces, parsley sprigs, or carrot curls.

Chapter Nine

TOSSED SALAD

½ head lettuce, cut into bite size pieces
2 medium tomatoes, cut into thin wedges
6 green salad onions, sliced
1 large cucumber, peeled and sliced
1 cup sliced radishes

Toss all vegetables together gently and serve with desired salad dressing.

Serves 4-6

VEGETABLE SALAD

1 head cauliflower, chopped
1 bunch broccoli, chopped
3 carrots, sliced
2 cucumbers, sliced
2 cups radishes, sliced
1 small onion, sliced

Gently toss vegetables together. Top with desired dressing.

Serves 6-8

SPINACH SALAD

8 ounces spinach, torn into bite-sized pieces
1 can (16 ounces) bean sprouts, drained
1 can (8 ounces) water chestnuts, drained and sliced
1 cup CROUTONS

Toss spinach, bean sprouts, and water chestnuts. Sprinkle with CROUTONS, and serve with desired salad dressing.

Serves 4-6

THREE BEAN SALAD

2 cups cut wax beans
2 cups green beans
2 cups kidney beans
½ cup chopped green peppers
1 small onion sliced into thin rings
¼ cup light corn syrup
⅔ cup lemon juice
⅓ cup oil
1 teaspoon salt

Drain all beans. Combine and add green pepper and onion. Mix together corn syrup, lemon juice, and oil. Pour over beans. Add salt and toss. Chill overnight.

Serves 4-6

Chapter Nine

HOT 5 BEAN SALAD

¼ cup oil
⅓ cup corn syrup
2 tablespoons cornstarch
1 ½ teaspoons salt
¾ cup lemon juice
½ cup water
1 teaspoon salt
1 teaspoon onion powder
½ teaspoon garlic powder

In large skillet combine oil, corn syrup, cornstarch, and salt. Stir in lemon juice and water. Cook until boiling. Remove from heat and add the following ingredients:

2 cups red kidney beans
2 cups green beans
1 ½ cups lima beans
2 cups wax beans
2 cups garbanzo beans
½ cup imitation bacon bits (optional)

Mix ingredients. Return skillet to heat, cover and simmer 10-15 minutes.

Serves 6-8

BROCCOLI SALAD

2 bunches of broccoli, cut into bite-sized pieces
2 medium red onions, sliced thin
2 tablespoons imitation bacon pieces
3 cups MAYONNAISE
3 tablespoons lemon juice

Mix broccoli, onions, and bacon pieces together. Blend mayonnaise and lemon juice thoroughly. Fold dressing into vegetable mixture and refrigerate for 2 hours.

Serves 4-6

CUCUMBER ONION SALAD

2 medium cucumbers, peeled and sliced
2 medium onions, sliced thin
1 cup MAYONNAISE
2 tablespoons lemon juice

Place cucumbers in a shallow dish, sprinkle with salt. Let stand overnight. In the morning, drain cucumbers and rinse. Let dry. Mix onions with cucumbers. Beat together with a fork the MAYONNAISE and lemon juice. Stir into mixed cucumbers and onions.

Serves 4-6

Chapter Nine

ZUCCHINI TOSS

1 small bunch romaine, torn into pieces
2 tablespoons olive oil
1 medium zucchini, thinly sliced
½ cup radishes, sliced
1 clove garlic, crushed
3 green onions, sliced
1 tablespoon lemon juice
½ teaspoon salt

Toss romaine and oil until leaves glisten. Add remaining ingredients; toss.

Serves 4

COLESLAW

1 ½ cup shredded purple cabbage
2 cups shredded yellow cabbage
¼ cup shredded carrots
2 cups BASIC SAUCE
¼ teaspoon salt
¼ teaspoon onion powder
¼ cup pickle relish

Mix all ingredients well and chill before serving.

Serves 4

HAWAIIAN COLESLAW

1 small head red cabbage, shredded
1 cup drained, crushed pineapple
2 carrots, grated
2 green onions, finely chopped
½ teaspoon salt
½ cup MAYONNAISE

Mix together all ingredients and refrigerate for several hours.

Serves 4-6

GARDEN STUFFED TOMATOES

Cut tomatoes in cups or daisies. When ready to serve salt cut surfaces and fill with desired filling.

CUP: Cut thin slice from top, scoop out center invert and chill.

DAISY: Turn tomato stem side down. Cut down not quite through in 5 or 6 wedges. Scoop out small amount of center, invert and chill.

FILLING IDEAS: chilled Spanish rice, grated lettuce, sliced olives, small pieces of chopped tomato mixed with MAYONNAISE, cooked frozen peas.

Chapter Nine

AVOCADO BOWL

Tear 1 small head of lettuce into bite size pieces and place in a salad bowl. Peel 2 avocados and slice into wedges. Arrange avocado wedges around the edge of the bowl. Fill center with 1 cup of mixed grapefruit and orange sections.

Serves 4

MACARONI SALAD

1 cup elbow macaroni, cooked, drained, and cooled
½ celery, sliced thin
¼ cup green salad onions, sliced
¼ cup pickle relish
½ cup olives, sliced
¼ teaspoon salt
1 cup MAYONNAISE
1 tablespoon pimento (optional)

Mix together all ingredients adding MAYONNAISE last. Chill.

Serves 2-4

POTATO SALAD

3 cups MAYONNAISE
6 medium potatoes, cooked in peels, cooled, then peeled and cubed
1 cup celery, sliced thin
1/4 cup onion, chopped
1 cup black olives, sliced
1 teaspoon celery seed
1/2 teaspoon salt
2 tablespoons pimento (optional)

Combine potatoes, celery, onion, and olives. When ready to serve add chilled MAYONNAISE, salt, and celery seed. Mix carefully.

Serves 4-6

Chapter Nine

HOT POTATO SALAD

4 medium potatoes, cut into halves
2 tablespoons imitation bacon bits
1 medium onion, chopped
1 tablespoon flour
1 tablespoon sugar
1 teaspoon salt
1/4 teaspoon celery seed
1 cup water
1/4 cup lemon juice

Heat to boiling 2 cups water and 1 teaspoon salt. Add potatoes, reduce heat, cover and cook until tender, 20 to 25 minutes. Drain and cool. Saute onion until tender in 2 tablespoons vegetable oil. Stir in flour, sugar, salt, and celery seed. Cook over low heat, stirring constantly, until mixture is smooth. Stir in water and lemon juice. Heat to boiling, stirring constantly. Boil and stir 1 minute; remove from heat. Add imitation bacon bits to hot mixture, then slice in warm potatoes. Cook until hot and bubbly, stirring gently.

Serves 2-4

TACO SALAD

¼ green pepper, minced
1 green onion, finely chopped
3 tablespoons olive oil
1 tablespoon lemon juice
¼ teaspoon salt
½ head green leaf lettuce, washed and broken into bite-size pieces
1 cup black olives, sliced
2 tomatoes, diced
1 cup broken tortilla chips or corn chips
1 cup GUACAMOLE (optional)

Make the dressing in a small bowl by mixing the green pepper, green onion, olive oil, lemon juice, and salt. Whisk and allow to stand for 30 minutes. In a large salad bowl mix the lettuce, sliced olives, tomato, and tortilla chips. Cover with the dressing and toss. Serve with GUACAMOLE if desired.

Serves 4

MANDRIN CITRUS COCONUT BOWL

Combine 1 ½ cups pineapple tidbits, drained, 1 cup mandrin oranges, drained, 1 cup green seedless grapes, and 1 cup flaked coconut. Chill several hours. Serve on lettuce leaves.

Serves 2-4

Chapter Nine

WALDORF SALAD

2 cups diced apples
¼ cup celery, sliced thin
½ cup walnuts, chopped
1 cup miniature Kosher marshmallows (optional)
1 tablespoon corn syrup
½ teaspoon lemon juice
dash salt
¾ cup WHIPPED TOPPING

Mix all ingredients together and chill for 1 hour before serving.

Serves 4

DELICIOUS GOLDEN FRUIT DISH

3 large Golden Delicious apples
4 large ripe bananas
1 ½ cups unsweetened crushed pineapple
½ cup undiluted frozen orange juice, unsweetened
½ cup flaked coconut

Dice apples. Slice the bananas. Stir all ingredients together and chill.

Serves 4-6

AMBROSIA

3/4 cup diced oranges
2 bananas, peeled and sliced
1/2 cup seedless green grapes
1/4 cup pitted dates, cut into small pieces
3 tablespoons pineapple juice
1/4 cup flaked coconut
1/2 cup orange juice

Combine fruits, mix together well. Pour juices over fruit, mix and chill. Top with coconut.

Serves 4

APPLE SALAD

8 cups shredded apples
4 cups oranges, chopped fine
1/2 cup chopped walnuts
2 cups WHIPPED TOPPING (optional)

Mix all ingredients and chill.

Serves 4-6

Salad Dressing

SALAD DRESSINGS

Celery Seed Dressing	265
Cucumber Dressing	264
Florida Dressing	264
Italian Dressing	262
Low Calorie Tomato Dressing	265
Sesame Tahini Dressing	267
Spicy Italian Dressing	263
Sunflower Oil-Free Dressing	267
Sweet-Sour Dressing	266
Thousand Island Dressing	262
Tofu Dressing	266
Tomato Dressing	263

Notes

Chapter Ten

THOUSAND ISLAND DRESSING

1 cup MAYONNAISE
1/4 cup tomato sauce
1 teaspoon cumin
1 teaspoon minced onion
1/4 teaspoon garlic salt
2 tablespoons minced green pepper
2 tablespoons minced celery
1/2 teaspoon salt

Mix all ingredients together well. Chill.

Makes about 1 1/2 cups

ITALIAN DRESSING

1 cup vegetable oil
1/3 cup lemon juice
1/4 teaspoon salt
1/4 teaspoon garlic powder
1/4 teaspoon onion powder

Mix all ingredients together and chill if desired.

Makes about 1 1/3 cups

Salad Dressings

SPICY ITALIAN DRESSING

1 cup vegetable oil
1/3 cup lemon juice
1 teaspoon corn syrup
1/2 teaspoon salt
1/2 teaspoon celery salt
1/4 teaspoon cumin
1 clove garlic, minced

Combine all ingredients in a jar, cover, shake and mix well. Chill.

Makes about 1 1/3 cups

TOMATO DRESSING

1/3 cup oil
1 1/2 cups tomatoes, peeled and diced
1/3 cup lemon juice
1/2 teaspoon onion powder
1/2 teaspoon garlic powder
1/2 teaspoon Italian seasoning

Blend all ingredients in a blender until smooth. Chill.

Makes about 2 cups

Chapter Ten

CUCUMBER DRESSING

1 cup cucumbers, peeled and diced
½ pound tofu
1 cup green onions, sliced
¼ cup water
⅛ cup lemon juice
1 tablespoon fresh parsley, chopped
½ teaspoon salt
Dash garlic powder

Seeds my be scraped out of cucumber if desired by first slicing cucumber in half lengthwise and scooping out with a spoon. Blend cucumber, tofu, and water in blender until smooth. Add remaining ingredients and mix well. Chill.

Makes about 2 cups

FLORIDA DRESSING

1 cup oil
1 cup lemon juice
1 teaspoon salt

Place all ingredients in a bowl and beat with a wire whisk. Chill.

Makes 2 cups

Salad Dressings

CELERY SEED DRESSING

1/3 cup corn syrup
1 teaspoon paprika
1 teaspoon celery seed
1/4 teaspoon salt
1/3 cup lemon juice
1 teaspoon minced onion
1 cup salad oil

Mix dry ingredients. Blend in syrup, lemon juice, and onion. Mix well. Add oil and beat with wire whisk. Chill.

Makes about 1 2/3 cups

LOW CALORIE TOMATO DRESSING

1 cup tomato sauce
2 tablespoons lemon juice
1 teaspoon soy sauce
1/2 teaspoon each: salt, dill weed, dried crushed basil

Mix all ingredients together and chill.

Makes about 1 cup

Chapter Ten

TOFU DRESSING

1 1/2 cup mashed tofu
1/3 cup water
1/4 cup lemon juice
2 tablespoons oil
1 teaspoon onion powder
1/4 teaspoon garlic powder
1 1/2 teaspoon McKay's chicken style seasoning (optional)
1 teaspoon salt
1 1/2 tablespoons pimento
1/4 cup olives, sliced thin
2 teaspoons chives

Blend first 8 ingredients in a blender until smooth. Stir in remaining ingredients. Chill.

Makes about 2 cups

SWEET-SOUR DRESSING

1/2 cup vegetable oil
2 tablespoons sugar
2 tablespoons lemon juice
1 tablespoon snipped parsley
1/2 teaspoon salt

Shake all ingredients in tightly covered jar. Chill before serving.

Makes about 1/2 cup

Salad Dressings

SUNFLOWER OIL-FREE DRESSING

3/4 cup sunflower seeds
2 1/2 cups water
3/4 cup rice (cooked and chilled)
2 teaspoons onion powder
1 1/2 teaspoons salt
2 teaspoons corn syrup
1/4 teaspoons garlic powder
dill seed and sweet basil

Blend rice and seeds with small amount of water until very smooth. Add remaining water and remaining ingredients blend again until mixed. Chill.

Makes about 3 cups

SESAME TAHINI DRESSING

3/4 cup tahini
1 1/2 tablespoons soy sauce
4 1/2 tablespoons water
3 tablespoons lemon juice

Mix all the ingredients until emulsified. Put into a dispenser bottle. Use on vegetables, beans, potatoes, breads or salads.

Makes about 1 cup

Desserts

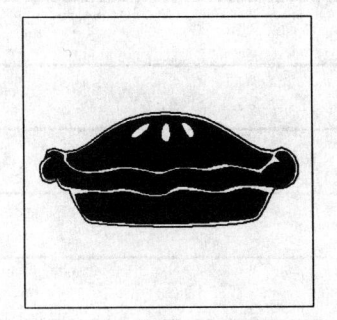

DESSERTS

Ambrosia Tapioca	296
Apple Banana Split	298
Apple Crisp	286
Apple Dumplings	297
Apple Pie	278
Apple Strudel	287
Banana Coconut Cream Pie	284
Banana Cream Pie	283
Blueberry Pie	279
Carob Pudding	293
Cashew Cookies	289
Cashew Cream	302
Cashew Pudding	294
Cherry Pie	280
Classic Pie Crust	274
Coconut Cashew Bars	291
Crisp Topping	277
Easy-do Pie Crust	276
Golden Fruit Nectar	296
Granola Bars	292
Lemon Pie	282

Maple Walnut Cream	300
Millet Pudding	294
Oat-Wheat Pie Crust	277
Oatmeal Cookies	290
Peach Pie	285
Peanut Butter Cookies	289
Pear Cobbler	288
Pineapple-Lemon Sauce	302
Powdered Coconut	297
Pumpkin Crisp	286
Pumpkin Pie	281
Rice Pudding	293
Smoothie	299
Strawberry Milk Shake	299
Sweet Potato Pie	278
Tofu Pudding	295
Vanilla Pudding	295
Vegetarian Whipped Cream	301
Whipped Topping	300
Whole Wheat Pie Crust, Double	275

Chapter Eleven

SWEETENERS

There are several types of sweeteners that can be used in cooking. In this cookbook we have used granulated sugar, brown sugar, corn syrup, Karo syrup, and maple syrup. For those wishing to use other types of sweeteners, you may need to do a little bit of experimenting, or just simply replace one type of sweetener for another. Below is a list of different sweeteners available.

GRANULATED SUGAR is a basic sweetener made from sugar cane or sugar beets.

POWDERED SUGAR is granulated sugar crushed and screened until grains are tiny. Starch is then added to keep lumping to a minimum.

BROWN SUGAR is a less refined form of granulated sugar. It derives a special flavor and moistness from the molasses that clings to the granules.

HONEY is made by bees from the nectar of flowers. It is sweeter than sugar. I do not use honey in this book as I am being sensitive to a 100% vegan market. Some vegans consider honey to be an animal product.

SYRUPS include corn, cane, sorghum, maple and molasses.

Desserts

PIE MAKING TIPS

Pie making will be much easier with the following equipment: a pastry blender to cut in shortening, a rolling pin, and a pastry cloth (to prevent pastry from sticking). Use a glass pie plate or a dull metal pie plate. Cool baked pies on a wire rack. The rack allows air to circulate under the pie and helps prevent the crust from becoming soggy.

A perfect pastry comes from accurate measuring. Gently spoon flour into a dry measuring cup and level off the top with a spatula. To measure solid shortening, pack it into a dry measuring cup and run a spatula through it to remove air pockets. To measure water for pastry, fill a measuring spoon to the top. Sprinkle 1 tablespoon at a time over flour mixture.

Roll pastry from the center to the edge lightly with even strokes, forming a circle about 12 inches in diameter about 1/8 inch thick. The pastry will transfer easier to the pie plate if it is wrapped around the rolling pin. Loosely unroll the pastry onto a 9-inch pie plate.

If the pastry is baked without a filling, prick the bottom and sides all over with a fork. This helps prevent crust from puffing up.

To prevent excessive browning of the edge of the pastry, cover with foil. If your pie is to bake less than 30 minutes foil is not needed.

To avoid messy spills in the oven when baking fruit pies, set the pie plate on a baking sheet on the oven rack. The pan will catch spills that bubble over.

Cream pies need to be thoroughly cooled before serving. After cooling to room temperature (about 4-6 hours), cover and refrigerate.

Chapter Eleven

CLASSIC PIE CRUST

8 OR 9-INCH SINGLE CRUST

1 1/3 cups all-purpose flour
1/2 teaspoon salt
1/2 cup vegetable shortening
3 tablespoons cold water
Follow instructions below.

8 OR 9-INCH DOUBLE CRUST

2 cups all-purpose flour
1 teaspoon salt
3/4 cup vegetable shortening
5 tablespoons cold water
Follow instructions below.

Combine flour and salt in bowl. Cut in vegetable shortening using pastry blender until all flour is blended in to form pea size chunks. Sprinkle on water, one tablespoon at a time. Toss lightly with fork until dough will form a ball.

FOR SINGLE CRUST press dough ball between hands to form 5 to 6 inch "pancake". Flour rolling surface and pin lightly. Roll dough into circle. Loosen dough carefully and place in pie pan. For recipe calling for baked pie shell, heat oven to 425 degrees. Thoroughly prick bottom and sides with fork to prevent shrinkage. Bake for 10 to 15 minutes or until lightly browned.

FOR DOUBLE CRUST divide dough in half. Roll each crust separately and transfer to pie plate. Add desired filling to unbaked pie shell. Roll top crust and lift onto filled pie. Trim. Fold top edge under bottom crust and flute. Cut slits in top crust or prick with fork. Bake according to filling recipe.

WHOLE WHEAT PIE CRUST, DOUBLE

2 1/4 cups whole wheat pastry flour
1/4 teaspoon salt
6 tablespoons vegetable oil
5 to 8 tablespoons ice water

Place all of the ingredients in the freezer for 1 hour before making the crust. Sift together the flour and salt. Quickly cut in the oil using a fork or a pastry cutter. Quickly sprinkle on ice water, a tablespoon at a time. Add only enough water to allow the dough to hold together for rolling. Do not overwork the dough. Cut the dough into two pieces. Put one piece between two sheets of waxed paper and roll into a circle about 1 inch larger than the pie pan, all around. Remove one sheet of waxed paper and invert the pie pan over the center of the dough. Place your hand under the dough and waxed paper and turn the pan right side up. Without removing the waxed paper, press the dough into place. Remove the paper. Fill the pie. Repeat rolling directions for second piece of dough for top crust. Place crust on top of filled pie. Crimp the edges to seal. Make a few holes in the top crust for venting. Bake as directed for the recipe you are using.

Chapter Eleven

EASY-DO PIE CRUST

8 OR 9-INCH SINGLE CRUST

1 1/8 cup white flour
1/3 cup vegetable oil
1/2 teaspoon salt
2 to 3 tablespoons cold water
Follow instructions below

8 OR 9-INCH DOUBLE CRUST

1 3/4 cup white flour
1/2 cup vegetable oil
1 teaspoon salt
3 to 4 tablespoons cold water
Follow instructions below

Mix flour, oil and salt until particles are size of small peas. Sprinkle in water, 1 tablespoon at a time, mixing until all flour is moistened. (If pastry seems dry, 1 to 2 tablespoons oil can be added. Do not add water.) Gather pastry into a ball.

FOR SINGLE CRUST PIE shape pastry into flattened round. Place flattened round between two 15-inch lengths of waxed paper. Wipe table with damp cloth to prevent paper from slipping. Roll pastry 2 inches larger than inverted pie plate. Peel off top paper. Place pastry paper side up in plate. Peel off paper. Ease pastry loosely into plate. Poke crust many times with a fork for venting, bake in oven at 400 degrees until lightly browned. Cool before filling.

FOR DOUBLE CRUST PIE divide pastry dough into halves, then roll top crust in same way as bottom crust. Cut slits in top pastry for steam to escape.

Desserts

OAT-WHEAT PIE CRUST

¾ cup white flour
¾ cup oat flour
½ cup whole wheat flour
1 teaspoon salt
⅔ cup oil
⅓ cup water

Make oat flour by blending dry rolled oats in the blender. Mix dry ingredients, then add oil and water. Roll between 2 layers of waxed paper or plastic wrap. Place in a pie pan. Prick with a fork, and bake at 350 degrees for 15 minutes or until lightly brown for pies requiring pre-cooked pie shell.

CRISP TOPPING

2 cups rolled oats
1 cup flour
¼ cup oil
½ teaspoon salt
1 teaspoon vanilla
3 tablespoons maple syrup
¼ cup water

Mix all ingredients well. Place desired amount of fruit into a baking dish. Sprinkle topping evenly over fruit mixture. Bake at 375 degrees for 45 minutes.

Chapter Eleven

APPLE PIE

6 cups tart apples, peeled and thinly sliced
1/2 cup sugar
1/2 cup unsweetened apple juice concentrate
4 tablespoons white flour
1 1/2 teaspoons coriander
Dash of salt
Pastry for double crust

Heat oven to 425 degrees. Prepare pastry. Mix sugar, flour, coriander and salt. Stir in apples. Stir thawed apple juice concentrate into apple mixture. Turn into a pastry-lined pie plate. Cover with top crust. Cut several slits in top crust, seal and flute. Cover edge with 3-inch strip of aluminum foil; remove foil during last 15 minutes of baking. Bake until crust is brown and juice begins to bubble through slits in crust, 40 to 50 minutes.

SWEET POTATO PIE

4 large sweet potatoes, baked and peeled
3/4 cup sugar or corn syrup (optional)
1 teaspoon coriander
2/3 cup soy milk
1/2 teaspoon salt
Pastry for single crust pie

Mash sweet potatoes until smooth. Add sugar, coriander, and soy milk to sweet potatoes and mix well. Put potato mixture into pastry lined 9-inch pie plate and bake in oven at 350 degrees for 45 minutes.

BLUEBERRY PIE

UNBAKED 9-INCH PIE CRUST

FILLING
2/3 cup sugar
3 tablespoons cornstarch
1/8 teaspoon salt
1/4 cup water
5 cups fresh blueberries
1 1/2 teaspoon lemon juice

Heat oven to 425 degrees. For filling, combine sugar, cornstarch, salt, water and 3 cups of the blueberries in saucepan. Cook on medium heat until mixture thickens and begins to boil. Remove from heat and cool slightly. Place remaining 2 cups of berries in unbaked pie shell. Stir lemon juice into cooked filling. Spoon cooked filling over fresh berries. Cover with top crust. Fold top edge under bottom crust. Flute edge with fork. Cut slits in top crust for steam to escape. Bake 30 to 40 minutes. Cool slightly before serving.

Chapter Eleven

CHERRY PIE

UNBAKED 9-INCH PIE CRUST

FILLING
1 cup sugar
1/3 cup all-purpose flour
1/8 teaspoon salt
1/4 teaspoon coriander
3 1/2 cups fresh or frozen dry pack pitted red tart cherries

Heat oven to 425 degrees. For filling, combine sugar, flour, salt, coriander and cherries in a bowl. Mix well. Spoon into unbaked pie shell. Moisten pastry edge with water. Cover with top crust. Fold top edge under bottom crust. Flute with fingers. Cut slits in top crust. Bake for 40 to 45 minutes. Cool slightly before serving.

Desserts

PUMPKIN PIE

UNBAKED 9-INCH SINGLE CRUST

FILLING
1 can (16 ounces) pumpkin
¾ cup sugar
½ teaspoon salt
1 ½ teaspoon coriander
1 ²⁄₃ cups soy milk
4 tablespoons cornstarch

Heat oven to 425 degrees. Prepare pastry. Place all ingredients except cornstarch and 6 tablespoons soy milk in a bowl and beat with a hand beater until well blended. Mix the cornstarch with the reserved 6 tablespoons of soy milk, then add to pumpkin mixture. Pour pumpkin mixture into pastry-lined pie plate. Bake 15 minutes. Reduce oven temperature to 350 degrees. Bake 45 minutes longer. Cool and serve with WHIPPED TOPPING.

Chapter Eleven

LEMON PIE

9-INCH BAKED PIE CRUST

1 cup sugar
2/3 cup cornstarch
3 cups water
1 teaspoon lemon extract
1 cup lemon juice
2 drops yellow food color (optional)

Mix sugar and cornstarch in saucepan. Stir in water gradually. Cook over medium heat, stirring constantly, until mixture thickens and boils. Boil and stir 1 minute. Remove from heat; stir in lemon juice and food color. Pour into pie shell. Cool at room temperature for 1 hour, then refrigerate until chilled. Serve with WHIPPED TOPPING.

Desserts

BANANA CREAM PIE

9-INCH BAKED PIE CRUST

1 1/2 cups cashews
3 cups water
1/3 cup light corn syrup
1 1/2 teaspoon vanilla
1/2 teaspoon salt
8 tablespoons cornstarch

Blend all ingredients in blender until smooth. Add 1 more cup of water and blend again. Pour mixture into cooking pot and cook over low heat until thick. Cool for 10 minutes. Slice 2 bananas on bottom of pie crust then pour cooked cream pie mixture over bananas. Cool at room temperature for 1 hour. Then refrigerate until well chilled. Slice 2 more bananas on top of pie and cover with WHIPPED TOPPING before serving.

Chapter Eleven

BANANA COCONUT CREAM PIE

9-INCH BAKED PIE CRUST

5 tablespoons cornstarch
3 cups soy milk
3 teaspoons corn syrup
2 teaspoons vanilla
4 tablespoons shredded coconut
3 ripe, but not brown bananas

Combine all ingredients except bananas in a blender and blend until creamy, about 3 minutes. Bring mixture to a boil in a saucepan, stirring constantly, lower heat, cook for 3 minutes, continue stirring to prevent scorching. Cool for 15 minutes. While cream is cooling, slice two bananas and arrange them evenly over the bottom of the crust. Cover the bananas with the cooled cream. Slice the remaining banana. Sprinkle slices with lemon juice to prevent darkening, then arrange slices on top of cream. Cool at room temperature for 1 hour, then cover and refrigerate until completely chilled.

Desserts

PEACH PIE

UNBAKED 9-INCH DOUBLE CRUST

FILLING
¾ cup sugar
¼ cup flour
¼ teaspoon coriander
6 cups sliced fresh peaches
1 teaspoon lemon juice

Heat oven to 425 degrees. For filling, combine sugar, flour, coriander, peaches and lemon juice in large bowl. Spoon filling into unbaked pie shell. Moisten pastry edge with water. Cover with top crust. Fold top edge under bottom crust. Flute with fork. Cut slits in top crust for steam to escape. Bake for 40 to 45 minutes or until crust is golden brown. Cool to room temperature. Serve with VEGETARIAN WHIPPED CREAM.

Chapter Eleven

APPLE CRISP

4 cups sliced tart apples
$2/3$ cup packed brown sugar
$1/2$ cup white flour
$1/2$ cup oats
1 teaspoon coriander
$1/3$ cup oil

Heat oven to 375 degrees. Arrange apples in greased square pan. Mix remaining ingredients; sprinkle over apples. Bake until topping is golden brown and apples are tender, about 30 minutes. Serve warm.

PUMPKIN CRISP

3 cups pumpkin
2 cups soy milk
$1/4$ teaspoon salt
4 tablespoons cornstarch
$1/2$ cup orange juice concentrate
$1/2$ cup coconut
$1/4$ cup sugar

Mix all ingredients until creamy. Place mixture in baking dish; top with CRISP TOPPING. Bake in oven at 350 degrees for 1 hour.

APPLE STRUDEL

1 1/2 cups pastry flour
1/4 teaspoon salt
1 tablespoon oil
1/3 to 1/2 cup water

To make dough, mix the flour and salt in a mixing bowl. Mix together oil and water. Mix dry ingredients with wet ingredients a small amount at a time of each. The dough should be soft and a little sticky, but not wet. If it is too dry, add more water, a little at a time. Knead dough for 10 minutes, cover with a warm towel, and set aside for 45 minutes.

3/4 cup raisins
3 tablespoons apple juice
3 medium-tart apples
2 tablespoons sugar
3/4 cup chopped walnuts

Place raisins in a small saucepan with apple juice. Boil and cook covered for several minutes. Peel the apples and cut into thin wedges. Cut the dough into two equal pieces. Place the first on a large piece of floured wax paper. Roll out very thin. Dip your fingers in a little oil and very lightly oil the dough. Sprinkle half of the sugar, raisins, apples, and walnuts over the dough, leaving a 1 inch border. Roll up the dough starting with the longer side. Moisten the seams with a little water and seal. Lift up the waxed paper and roll the strudel onto a lightly oiled baking sheet. Repeat for the second strudel. Preheat the oven to 400 degrees and bake for 30 minutes. Reduce heat to 350 degrees and bake for 10 minutes longer.

Chapter Eleven

PEAR COBBLER

6 medium ripe pears
2 tablespoons cornstarch
1 cup apple juice
2 tablespoons corn syrup
1/8 teaspoon salt
1/2 cup chopped walnuts
2 tablespoons vegetable oil
1/4 cup corn syrup
3/4 cup raw quick-cooking oats
1/3 cup pastry flour

Wash pears, cut them in half, remove the cores, and slice. In a small saucepan combine the cornstarch with 3 tablespoons of the apple juice and mix until smooth. Add the remaining apple juice, 2 tablespoons corn syrup, and salt. Heat until mixture becomes translucent and thick, stirring constantly. In a large bowl combine the pear slices, walnuts, and cornstarch mixture and turn it out into a baking dish. Preheat the oven to 350 degrees. Mix oats and flour with 1/4 cup corn syrup and oil until completely mixed. Crumble the oatmeal mixture evenly over the pears. Cover with foil and bake for 25 minutes. Uncover and bake for 10 minutes more.

Desserts

PEANUT BUTTER COOKIES

½ cup peanut butter
¼ cup Karo syrup
¼ cup sugar
¼ cup water
¼ teaspoon salt
½ teaspoon vanilla
1 ¼ cup white flour

Cream together all ingredients except flour until well mixed. Add flour. Form into balls, place balls on cookies sheet, then using fork flatten cookies with crisscrosses. Bake at 350 degrees for 20 minutes, or until lightly browned.

CASHEW COOKIES

1 cup sugar
½ cup vegetable oil
1 cup cashew nuts, ground
1 cup coconut
2 cups quick oats
½ cup pastry flour
½ teaspoon salt
½ cup soy milk

Cream together sugar, oil and ground cashews. Add coconut, oats, pastry flour and salt, mix well. Add soy milk and mix again. Shape into cookies and place on ungreased cookie sheet. Bake at 350 degrees for 20 to 25 minutes.

Chapter Eleven

OATMEAL COOKIES

1 cup oil
1 cup sugar
1 1/2 teaspoon vanilla
1 1/2 teaspoon salt
1 cup pastry flour
1/2 cup soy flour
1 cup cold water
5 cups rolled oats
3/4 cup chopped walnuts
1/2 cup raisins

Cream together oil, sugar, vanilla and salt. Add flours and water. Mix well. Add oats, nuts and raisins, mix well. Drop by the spoonful on greased cookie sheet. Flatten with fork. Bake until lightly browned, in oven at 350 degrees.

# COCONUT CASHEW BARS

1 cup light corn syrup
½ cup vegetable oil
2 tablespoons lemon juice
½ cup soy flour
2 cups quick oats
1 cup shredded coconut
1 cup ground cashews
¼ cup water
½ teaspoon vanilla
½ teaspoon salt
½ cup chopped walnuts
1 teaspoon coriander

Combine all ingredients and mix well. Press ¼ inch thick on oiled cookie sheet. Bake in oven at 350 degrees for 20 minutes. Cool 5 minutes then cut into squares. Let cool completely before removing from cookie sheet.

Chapter Eleven

GRANOLA BARS

¼ cup raisins
2 tablespoon apple juice
1 cup rolled oats
¼ cup chopped peanuts
¼ cup shredded coconut
2 tablespoons vegetable oil
2 tablespoon maple syrup
3 tablespoons peanut butter

In a small skillet heat the raisins and apple juice. Bring to a boil, remove from heat, cover, and let stand until raisins are plump. Combine the oats, peanuts, and coconut. Add the raisins and mix well. Heat the oil and maple syrup. Remove from heat and stir in the peanut butter. Pour the syrup mixture over the dry ingredients and mix well. Preheat the oven to 300 degrees. Press the batter into a greased and floured 9x13 inch loaf pan. Bake for 20 minutes, cool for 10 minutes, and cut into bars.

CAROB PUDDING

3 tablespoons cornstarch
2 tablespoons soy flour
3 tablespoons carob powder
1/4 teaspoon salt
1/4 cup karo syrup
1 3/4 cup soy milk
2 teaspoons vanilla
1/2 cup chopped nuts

Put all ingredients in blender except chopped nuts and blend until smooth. Put blended mixture into medium saucepan and heat until thick and bubbly. Cook over medium heat 5 minutes. Remove from heat and stir in nuts. Pour evenly into 4 small dessert dishes. Chill until cool.

RICE PUDDING

1 cup cooked RICE, chilled
1/3 cup maple syrup
1 can (13 1/4 ounces) crushed pineapple, drained
1/2 teaspoon vanilla
1/4 cup raisins
1/4 cup chopped walnuts

Mix all ingredients well. Place mixture in small saucepan and cook over medium heat just until warm, or serve cold if desired.

Chapter Eleven

CASHEW PUDDING

1 cup raw cashews
3 1/2 cups water
6 tablespoons cornstarch
1/2 cup maple syrup
1/4 teaspoon salt
1 1/2 teaspoons vanilla

Place the cashews and water in a blender and blend for 5 minutes. Strain the liquid through a very fine sieve and discard the pulp. Blend again. Mix the cornstarch with 4 tablespoons of cashew liquid until creamy. Place all the ingredients in a blender at high speed for 3 minutes, then place in a saucepan and bring to a boil, stirring constantly. Cook for 2 minutes. Chill and serve. Top with WHIPPED TOPPING.

MILLET PUDDING

2 cups cooked MILLET (use when warm)
1 cup pineapple juice
1/4 teaspoon salt
1 teaspoon vanilla
1/4 cup coconut
1 cup pineapple chunks
2 cups GRANOLA

Blend the first five ingredients together in a blender for 2 minutes. Stir in pineapple chunks. Line the bottom of a serving bowl with GRANOLA and pour millet mixture over GRANOLA. Serve warm or cold.

Desserts

VANILLA PUDDING

⅓ cup sugar
3 tablespoons cornstarch
⅛ teaspoon salt
2 cups soy milk
2 teaspoons vanilla

Mix sugar, cornstarch and salt in 2-quart saucepan. Stir in milk. Cook over medium heat, stirring constantly, until mixture thickens and boils. Boil and stir 1 minute. Remove from heat; stir in vanilla. Pour into dessert dishes. Cool slightly; refrigerate. Serve topped with VEGETARIAN WHIPPED CREAM.

TOFU PUDDING

2-16 ounce packages firm tofu, drained
1 cup unsweetened apple juice concentrate
¼ cup lemon juice
1½ teaspoon vanilla
⅔ cup grated coconut
4 bananas, ripe
1 pint fresh fruit, any kind, sliced

Combine the tofu, apple juice concentrate, and vanilla in a blender and blend until creamy. Add the coconut and blend for one minute longer. In a glass dish, layer the tofu mixture, bananas and fresh fruit. Top with the tofu mixture. Chill 2 hours.

Chapter Eleven

AMBROSIA TAPIOCA

½ cup sugar
¼ cup quick-cooking tapioca
Dash of salt
2 ½ cups orange juice
1 cup orange sections
¼ cup flaked coconut

Mix sugar, tapioca, salt and orange juice in 2-quart saucepan. Let stand 5 minutes. Heat to boiling over medium heat, stirring constantly. Cool slightly. Stir in orange sections and coconut. Refrigerate until cool.

GOLDEN FRUIT NECTAR

2 cups orange juice
2 cups pineapple juice
2 ripe bananas

Place all in blender and blend until smooth and creamy. Refrigerate unused nectar. Use as a cereal topping if desired.

Desserts

APPLE DUMPLINGS

Pastry for 9-inch double crust

6 baking apples, cored
3 tablespoons raisins
3 tablespoons chopped nuts
1 ½ cups maple syrup

Heat oven to 425 degrees. Prepare pastry as directed except-roll ⅔ into 14-inch square; cut into 4 squares. Roll remaining pastry into rectangle, 14x7 inches; cut into 2 squares. Place apple on each square. Mix raisins and nuts; fill each apple. Pour ¼ cup maple syrup in each apple. Moisten corners of pastry squares; bring 2 opposite corners up over apple and pinch. Repeat with remaining corners; pinch edges of pastry to seal. Place dumplings in ungreased oblong baking dish. Bake until apples are tender, about 40 minutes. Serve warm.

POWDERED COCONUT

½ cup grated dried coconut
½ cup date sugar

Mix the coconut and date sugar in a Moulinex grinder and grind until finely powdered. Sprinkle on french toast, toast with peanut butter, or fruit.

Chapter Eleven

APPLE BANANA SPLIT

1 large apple, peeled
2 tablespoons apple juice
1 large banana, peeled
1 cup MAPLE WALNUT CREAM
2 tablespoons chopped peanuts
4 fresh strawberries
2 tablespoons flaked coconut

Cut the apple in half and remove the core. In a saucepan, place the apple juice and then place the apple halves, flat side down. Cover and cook the apples at low heat for 10 minutes or until they are tender. Do not overcook. Place each apple flat side down on a dessert dish and spoon on remaining juice in saucepan. Chill covered for 2 hours. Cut the banana in half lengthwise and cut each piece in half through the middle. Place two banana slices, side-by-side, flat side down, on each plate. Lift each apple half and place it, flat side down, on top of the bananas. Spoon half of the MAPLE WALNUT CREAM over each apple. Sprinkle with the chopped nuts. Garnish with sliced strawberries and coconut.

Desserts

SMOOTHIE

3 chopped frozen bananas
½ cup pineapple juice
1 tablespoon orange juice concentrate
1 tablespoon apple juice concentrate

Place all ingredients in blender and blend until smooth.

Optional flavors to be mixed with bananas or used in place of bananas: Strawberries, Blueberries, Peaches, Cherries

STRAWBERRY MILK SHAKE

8 large ripe strawberries
1 ripe banana
2 cups RAW NUT MILK

Wash the strawberries, and place in a blender with the banana and NUT MILK. Blend until creamy.

Use your favorite fruits for new flavors.

Serves 2

Chapter Eleven

WHIPPED TOPPING

2 cups water
1/3 cup light corn syrup
1/2 cup white flour
1/2 teaspoon salt

Blend all ingredients until smooth. Put mixture in medium saucepan, cook over medium heat until thick, stirring constantly to prevent scorching. Put saucepan with mixture in refrigerator and chill. When chilled return mixture to blender, blend until creamy adding 1 teaspoon vanilla. Continue blending adding slowly 2/3 cup oil. Mixture will be thick and creamy. Chill and serve over pies or fruit.

* Note: You will need a heavy duty blender to blend mixture after it has been chilled! It is very thick.

MAPLE WALNUT CREAM

1 cup soy milk powder
1 cup water
1 1/2 teaspoon maple flavoring
1/4 cup ground walnuts
1/2 cup maple syrup

Blend together first 4 ingredients in blender until smooth. Slowly add maple syrup. Chill. Excellent over fruit or GRANOLA.

Desserts

VEGETARIAN WHIPPED CREAM

½ cup soy milk
½ teaspoon agar flakes
1 tablespoon water
2 teaspoons oil
1 teaspoon vanilla
1 teaspoon light corn syrup

Mix the soy milk, agar, and water in a saucepan and bring to a boil. Simmer, covered, for 5 minutes until the agar has dissolved. Stir several times. Pour the soy milk mixture into a measuring cup and add just enough water to make ½ cup. Refrigerate for 45 minutes. Combine the chilled soy milk mixture with the oil and vanilla and beat at high speed with an electric mixer. After about 3 minutes, slowly add the corn syrup. Beat for 6-8 minutes longer. Refrigerate unused portion.

Chapter Eleven

CASHEW CREAM

½ cup blanched cashews
½ cup water
¼ teaspoon salt
1 teaspoon vanilla
1 tablespoon corn syrup
2 teaspoons vegetable oil

Place the nuts and water in a blender and blend at high speed until smooth and creamy, about 10 minutes. Add remaining ingredients and blend for 1 minute. Refrigerate for 2 hours. Whip with an eggbeater for 1 minute before serving. Makes about 1 cup.

PINEAPPLE-LEMON SAUCE

1 cup cold pineapple juice
1 ½ tablespoons cornstarch
2 tablespoons lemon juice
⅓ cup light corn syrup

Mix cornstarch with pineapple juice and cook in a small saucepan over medium-low heat until thick. Remove from heat and add remaining ingredients. Use hot, or chill. Serve over fruit.

Four Week Meal Planner

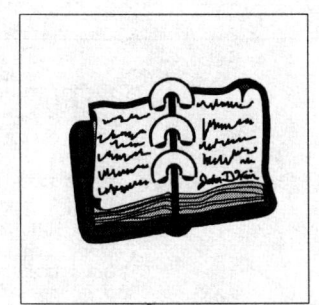

• Based on a two meal a day schedule •

Breakfast

Dinner

French toast
Thickened peaches
Apple wedges

Pecan herb loaf
Savory broccoli
Tossed salad
White bread
Creamy onion gravy

Corn meal mush
Hashbrowns
Fresh tomato slices
Oat gems

Split pea soup
Cucumber onion salad
Croutons

Crunchy granola
Grapefruit cup
Bananas
Whole wheat toast
Date butter

Baked Vegi-burgers
French fries
Sliced tomatoes and onions
Burger buns
Catsup and mayonnaise

Raw applesauce
Green grapes
Raisin bread
Almond butter

Savory millet patties/gravy
Harvard beets
Green beans
Tossed salad/salad dressing
Bread rolls

Breakfast   *Dinner*

Millet	Burritos
Pears	Spanish rice
Strawberries	Sour cream
Blueberry muffins	
Cashew butter	

Fruited oats	Lasagna
Applesauce	Italian corn
Oranges	Vegetable salad
Toast	Garlic toast
Peanut butter	

Delicious golden fruit dish	Lentil nut roast
Raisins	Chived carrots
Coconut chews	Spinach salad
	Bread rolls
	Seasoned gravy

Apple icing bread	Stuffed peppers
Pears	Carrots piquant
Strawberries	Celery sticks

Breakfast

Eggless omelet
Breakfast bars
Oranges

Rice fritters
Thickened blueberries
Bananas
Whole wheat toast
Almond butter

Granola
Fresh apple milk
Apples
Green grapes

Oat waffles
Thickened peaches
Raisins
Almonds

Dinner

Vegetarian steaks
Country bread stuffing
Harvard beets
Corn
Mrs. Tyler's gravy

Shepherd pie
Tossed salad/salad dressing
Rye bread

Pasta Primavera
Tomato slices
Garlic toast

Black beans
Steamed rice
Savory broccoli
Corn bread

Breakfast

Buckwheat-rice cereal
Oranges
Bananas
Whole wheat bread
Cashew butter

Mandrin citrus coconut bowl
Granola bars
Raisins

Multi-grain waffles
Thickened pears
Bananas

Swedish farina
Coconut milk
Oranges
Strawberries
Coconut chews

Dinner

Cashew garbanzo bake
Oven peas
Sliced tomatoes
White bread

Haystacks
Sour cream

Pizza
Tossed salad/salad dressing

Sun patties
Cooked carrots
Zucchini toss
Seasoned gravy

Breakfast

Dinner

Baked oatmeal
Apples
Green grapes

Cashew rice roast
Creole green beans
Vegetable salad
Bread rolls
Cashew gravy

Breakfast rice pudding
Oranges
Oat bread
Date nut spread

Italian lentils
Corn and onions
Spinach salad
Garlic toast

Grits
Hashbrowns
Cantaloupe
Whole wheat toast
Brown gravy

Beans and pasta
Tomato and cucumber slices
Whole wheat bread

Grapefruit cup
Raisins
Bananas
Coriander rolls

Potato corn chowder
Carrot and celery sticks
Croutons

Breakfast　　　　　*Dinner*

Fruit soup
Granola
Bananas

Minestrone
Bread rolls

Millet pudding
Oranges
Raisin bread
Apple butter

Tofu burgers
Macaroni salad
Tomato and onion slices
Burger buns
Mayonnaise and catsup

Oatmeal
Pretty pink applesauce
Green grapes
Banana bread

Navy bean soup
Coleslaw
Oat crackers

Pancakes
Thickened peaches
Apple wedges

Italian potato dumplings
Italian corn
Tossed salad/salad dressing
Garlic toast

Breakfast

Grits
Hashbrowns
Tomato and onion slices
Whole wheat toast

Crunchy granola
Maple walnut milk
Bananas
Oranges
Coriander rolls

Crepes
Thickened apples and raisins
Strawberries
Maple walnut cream

Baked Oatmeal
Strawberry Date Milk
Coconut Chews

Dinner

Vegetable chow mein
Fried rice
Chow mein noodles

Macaroni and chee
Peppered zucchini
Cucumber slices
Bread rolls

Lentil nut roast
Chived carrots
Avocado bowl
White bread

Stuffed Manicotti
Green peas
Tossed Salad
Italian Dressing
Bread Rolls

SUBSTITUTIONS

If you don't have:	Substitute:
1 tablespoon cornstarch	2 tablespoons flour
1 package active dry yeast	1 cake compressed yeast
1 cup granulated sugar	1 cup brown sugar or 2 cups sifted powdered sugar
1 cup corn syrup	1 cup granulated sugar plus $1/4$ cup liquid
2 cups tomato sauce	$3/4$ cup tomato paste plus 1 cup water
1 clove garlic	$1/8$ teaspoon garlic powder
1 small onion	1 teaspoon onion powder

EGG SUBSTITUTES

There are several qualities of eggs that need to be replaced in the kitchen. Nutritionally the replacements are easily found. Whole grains, all common varieties of greens, and legumes will supply the nutritional needs usually obtained from eggs. The binding quality of eggs is provided by the yolk and is needed in certain types of loaves and roasts. The binding quality can generally be supplied by flour from any whole grain. Then, there is the leavening agency of the whites of eggs needed in certain quick breads. Flour such as soy or garbanzo flour will provide a leavening quality.

LEAVENING SUBSTITUTE: Flour made from any bland legume such as garbanzos or soybeans may be used for its slight leavening property. Try about two tablespoons per cup of other flour in the recipe. Use a little extra water as it absorbs water as it cooks. May be used in pancakes.

Mix equal quantities of soy flour and starch. Use about two tablespoons to replace one egg in a recipe. Add some extra water.

BINDER TO PREVENT BREAKING UP: Any whole grain or legume flour may be used as a binder. Starch gives an unusual binding agency with a crustiness outside. Use about 1-2 tablespoons to replace one egg.

COOKING TERMS

BEAT - To make a mixture smooth by adding air with a brisk whipping motion.

BLANCH - To precook in boiling water or steam to prepare foods for canning or freezing, or to loosen their skins.

BLEND - To thoroughly combine two or more ingredients by hand with a stirring motion to make a smooth mixture.

BOIL - To cook in liquid at boiling temperature where bubbles rise to the surface and break.

BREAD - To coat with bread crumbs before cooking.

BROIL - To cook by direct heat under a broiler.

CAN - To preserve food by sealing it in airtight containers. The food is processed in a water bath or pressure canner.

CHOP - To cut into pieces about the size of peas with a knife, chopper, or food processor.

COAT - To evenly cover food with crumbs or flour.

COOL - To remove from heat and let stand at room temperature.

CREAM - To beat a mixture with a spoon or electric mixer until it becomes soft and smooth.

CRISP-TENDER - To cook food to the point where it is tender but still crisp.

CUBE - To cut into pieces that are the same size on each size, about 1/2 inch.

CUT IN - To mix shortening with dry ingredients using a pastry blender or two knives.

DICE - To cut food into small cubes of uniform size, about 1/4 inch.

FINELY SHRED - To rub food across a fine shredding surface to form very narrow strips.

FREEZE - To reduce the temperature of foods so that they become solidified.

GARNISH - To decorate the served dish with small pieces of food that have attractive texture or color.

GRATE - To rub food across a grating surface that separates the food into very fine particles.

GRIND - To use a food grinder to cut food into fine pieces.

JULIENNE - To cut vegetables into matchlike strips.

KNEAD - To work dough with the heel of your hand in a pressing and folding motion.

MINCE - To chop food into very small, irregularly shaped pieces.

PEEL - To remove the outer layer or skin from a fruit or vegetable.

PIT - To remove the seed from a piece of fruit.

PRESERVE - To prepare fruits or vegetables for future use by salting, dehydrating, canning, or freezing.

PUREE - To use a blender or food processor to convert food into a liquid.

SAUTE' - To brown or cook food in a small amount of hot fat.

SCORE - To cut narrow grooves partway through the outer surface of a food.

SHRED - To rub food on a shredder to form long narrow pieces.

SIFT - To put one or more dry ingredients through a sifter to incorporate air and break up lumps.

SIMMER - To cook food in liquid over low heat where bubbles form at a slow rate and burst before reaching the surface.

STEAM - To cook food in steam, using a small amount of boiling water.

STEEP - To extract color or flavor from a substance by leaving it in liquid just below the boiling point.

STIR - To mix ingredients with a spoon in a circular motion until well combined.

TOSS - To mix ingredients lightly by lifting and dropping them with a spoon.

SIMPLE MEASURES

Dash or pinch	=	less than 1/8 teaspoon
3 teaspoons	=	1 tablespoon
2 tablespoons	=	1/8 cup
16 tablespoons	=	1 cup
1 cup	=	1/2 pint
2 cups	=	1 pint (1/2 quart)
4 cups	=	1 quart
16 fluid ounces	=	2 cups

Index

Breads

Breading Meal	27
BREADS	
Banana	20
Corn	14
Oat	15
One Loaf Recipe for Children	12
Raisin	18
Rye	16
White	11
Whole Wheat	10
Coconut Chews	26
CRACKERS	
Oat	23
Sesame	25
Croutons	27
Garlic Bread Chips	26
Garlic Toast	24
Hush Puppies	23
MUFFINS	
Apple-Date	19
Banana Bran	21
Blueberry	17
Oat Gems	24
ROLLS	
Bread	13
Coriander	22
Tortillas	25

Breakfast

Apple Icing Bread	36
Baked Apples	52
Baked Oatmeal	47
Breakfast Bars	53
Buckwheat-Rice Cereal	46
Corn Meal Mush	45
Crunchy Granola	49
Eggless Omelet	44
French Toast	35
FRUIT	
Juice Syrup	41
Medley	52
Sauce	34
Soup	54
Fruited Oats	46
Granola	48
Grapefruit Cup	53
Grits	45
Millet	43
PANCAKES	38
Corn Meal	40
Potato	39
Raw Applesauce	51
Rice Fritters	42
Rice Pudding	42
Sauteed Breakfast Apples	51
Scrambled Tofu	54
Spiced Apple and Raisin Sauce	50
Swedish Farina	50
WAFFLES	
Multi-Grain	36
Oat	37
Pecan Oat	37

Cheeses, Spreads and Condiments

Basic Sauce	186
BUTTERS	
Almond	190
Apple	190
Cashew	191
Date	191
Catsup	180
Chee Sauce	178
CHEESES	
Agar	174
Melty	176
Mock American	177
Pimento	175
Tasty Cheese Sauce	176
DIPS	
Cucumber	188
Cucumber Spinach	187
Eggplant	188
Golden Garbanzo	187
Parsley-Chive	189
Guacamole	183
Humus	185
Lemon and Oil Sauce	179
MAYONNAISE	181
Dill	181
Mayo Spread	182
Mustard	180
Relish	182
Salsa	179
Sesame Tahini	185
Sour Cream	184
SPREADS	
Date Nut	191
Mayo Spread	182
Party	183
Sandwich Spread	183
Tofu Sour Cream	184
Tomato Topping	178

Desserts

Ambrosia Tapioca	296
Apple Strudel	287
COBBLERS AND CRISPS	
Apple Crisp	286
Pear Cobbler	288
Pumpkin Crisp	286
Coconut Cashew Bars	291
COOKIES	
Cashew	289
Oatmeal	290
Peanut Butter	289
CRUST	
Classic Pie Crust	274
Crisp Topping	277
Easy-Do Pie Crust	276
Oat-Wheat Pie Crust	277
Whole Wheat Pie Crust, Double	275
FRUIT DESSERTS	
Apple Banana Split	298
Apple Dumplings	297
Golden Fruit Nectar	296
Gronola Bars	292
PIES	
Apple	278
Banana Coconut Cream	284
Banana Cream	283
Blueberry	279
Cherry	280
Lemon	282
Peach	285
Pumpkin	281
Sweet Potato	278

PUDDINGS
- Carob — 293
- Cashew — 294
- Millet — 294
- Rice — 293
- Tofu — 295
- Vanilla — 295

Smoothie — 299
Strawberry Milk Shake — 299

TOPPINGS
- Cashew Cream — 302
- Pineapple-Lemon Sauce — 302
- Maple Walnut Cream — 300
- Powdered Coconut — 297
- Vegetarian Whipped Cream — 301
- Whipped Topping — 300

Entrees

BEANS
- Baked — 123
- Beans and Greens — 129
- Beans and Pasta — 124
- Black — 128
- Black-Eyed Pea Potpourri — 125
- East India Black-Eyed Peas — 122
- Refried — 127
- Summer Squash and Beans — 93

BURGERS
- Baked Vegi — 114
- Oat — 118
- Tofu — 115

Burritos — 95
Cashew Rice Roast — 140

CASSEROLES
- Cabbage Casserole — 145
- Green Beans and Potato — 90
- Lentil Casserole — 135
- Lima Bean and Tomato — 126
- Split Peas and Rice Casserole — 131
- Zucchini — 92

Chili — 126
Chili-N-Grits — 104

CHINESE
- Chinese Pepper Steak — 136
- Sukiyaki — 137
- Vegetable Chow Mein — 138

Corn Tamale Pie — 96
Country Bread Stuffing — 106
Creole — 121
Crepes — 98
Fancy Mashed Potato Bake — 89

GARBANZO DISHES
- Cashew Garbanzo Bake — 120
- Garbanzo Pot Pie — 121
- Garbanzos and Pasta — 147
- Mexican Garbanzos — 122

Goulash — 146
Haystacks — 97
Hearty Hash — 88
Hoppin' John — 141
Italian Potato Dumplings — 105
Jambalaya — 139
Lasagna — 152

LENTIL DISHES
- Italian Lentils — 133
- Lentil Casserole — 135
- Lentil-Nut Roast — 131
- Lentils and Noodles — 134
- Sweet and Sour Lentils — 132

Lima Broccoli Bake — 130

LOAFS
- Carrot Rice Loaf — 143
- Oat — 118
- Pecan Herb — 86

Vegetarian Meat	100
Macaroni and Chee	144
Oat Crepes	99

PASTAS

Baked Macaroni	144
Beans and Pasta	124
Fri Chic and Pasta	149
Garbanzos and Pasta	147
Goulash	146
Lasagna	152
Lentils and Noodles	134
Macaroni and Chee	144
Pasta Primavera	150
Peppers and Pasta	148
Stuffed Manicotti	151
Vegetable Lasagna	153

PATTIES

Savory Millet	117
Split Pea	116
Sun	119

Pizza	102

POT PIES

Garbanzo	121
Potato	87
Shepherd Pie	101
Sunflower "Beefy"	108

RICE DISHES

Carrot Rice Loaf	143
Cashew Rice Roast	140
Fried Rice	141
Hoppin' John	141
Rice Medley	143
Spanish Rice	142
Split Peas and Rice Casserole	131

SPLIT PEA DISHES

Split Pea Patties	116
Split Peas and Rice Casserole	131

STEWS

Great Northern	112
Irish	110
Vegetable	111

STUFFED VEGETABLES

Stuffed Cabbage Rolls	107
Stuffed Peppers	90
Vegetable Stuffed Baked Potatoes	91
Zucchini Boats	94
Summer Squash and Beans	93
Tofu Meat Balls	100
Tostadas	101
Vegetarian Steaks	113
Walnut Balls	103

Gravies and Sauces

GRAVIES

Basic	159
Bean	159
Brown	160
Cashew	160
Creamy Onion	161
Holiday	161
Mrs. Tyler's	162
Sauteed	162
Seasoned	163
Sunflower	164

SAUCES

Bechamel	165
Chee	178
Garlic Tomato	167
Italian Tomato Sauce	169
Lemon and Oil	179
Onion	166
Seasoned Tomato	167
Spaghetti	168
Sweet and Sour	164
Tasty Cheese	176

Tomato Relish	166
White	165

Non-Dairy Milks

Almond	68
Cashew	67
Coconut	63
Fresh Apple	64
Madison	64
Maple Walnut	69
Raw Nut	63
Soy	65
Strawberry Date	67
Walnut	66

Salad Dressings

Celery Seed	265
Cucumber	264
Florida Dressing	264
Italian	262
Low Calorie Tomato	265
MAYONNAISE	
Dill	181
Mayo Spread	182
Mayonnaise	181
Sesame Tahini	267
Spicy Italian	263
Sunflower Oil-Free	267
Sweet-Sour	266
Thousand Island	262
Tofu	266
Tomato	263

Salads

Avocado Bowl	252
Coleslaw	250
Coleslaw, Hawaiian	251
FRUIT	
Ambrosia	257
Apple	257
Delicious Golden Fruit Dish	256
Mandrin Citrus Coconut Bowl	255
Waldorf	256
Garden Stuffed Tomatoes	251
Macaroni Salad	252
Taco Salad	255
Tossed Salad	246
VEGETABLE	
Broccoli	249
Cucumber Onion	249
Hot 5 Bean	248
Hot Potato	254
Potato	253
Spinach	247
Three Bean	247
Vegetable Salad	246
Zucchini Toss	250

Seasonings

Home Made Chicken Seasoning	192
Seasoned Salt	192

Soups

Barley Soup	224
Black Bean Soup	227

Celery Chowder	238
Chicken Noodle Soup	236
Cream of Tomato Soup	233
Elegant Potato Soup	230
French Onion Soup	230
Gazpacho	231
Lentil Parsnip Soup	226
Macaroni Soup	232
Meaty Rice Soup	232
Minestrone	234
Navy Bean Soup	224
Northern Bean Soup	225
Oriental Soup	229
Potato Corn Chowder	237
Split Pea Soup	228
Vegetable Broth	238
Vegetable Cream Soup	233
Vegetable Soup	235
Vegetable Stock	239

Vegetables

Beets, Glazed	215
Beets, Harvard	214
BROCCOLI	
Italian	209
Savory	209
With Chee Sauce	209
Cabbage, Braised	203
Cabbage, Oriental	203
CARROTS	
Chived	211
Creamed	210
Piquant	210
Cauliflower Medley	208
Cauliflower, Saucy	208
Corn and Onions	212

Corn, Italian	212
Corn Pot Pie	213
Creamed Vegetables	211
Eggplant, Scalloped	204
Green Beans and Tomatoes	206
Green Beans, Creole	206
Limas, Country	205
Peas, Oven	213
POTATOES	
Croquettes	217
French Fries	216
Mashed Potato Bake	216
Scalloped	218
Spinach	219
Sweet Potato Bake	219
Sweet Potato Croquettes	217
Tomatoes, Baked Stuffed	207
Zucchini, Peppered	204

Info

BREAD	
Common Defects of Bread	6
Shaping Dinner Rolls	9
Yeast Breads	4
Breakfast	32
Calcium	62
Cereal	33
COOKING DIRECTIONS	
Beans	76
Pasta	79
Rice	77
Cooking Terms	313
Cooking Vegetables	198
Dairy Product Substitutes	60
Dextrinized Grains	32
Does Your Cooking Taste Flat?	XIV

Egg Substitutes	312
Fats	85
Food Storage	XV
Four Week Planner	303
Irritating Seasonings	83
Is Your Food Attractive	X
Is Your Food Palatable	IX
Making Foods Attractive	XII
Nuts	78
Pasta	79
Pie Making Tips	273
Proteins and B-Vitamins	84
Rice	80
Seasoning Guide	81
Simple Measures	316
Substitutions	311
Sweeteners	272
Two Meal Plan	VIII
Vegetables	202
Vitamin Sources	XVI

Thank you for purchasing DISTINCTIVE VEGETARIAN CUISINE. We hope you find it enjoyable. If you are interested in being on our mailing list so that you can be informed of future titles, please fill out the card below and mail it to:

Weir Writings
P.O. Box 10497
Spokane, Washington 99209

We are already putting together a mini-cookbook filled with vegan tofu recipes. If you have any suggestions on certain types of recipes you would enjoy in a vegan cookbook, feel free to send your suggestions to Weir Writings.

We look forward to serving you.

Sue M. Weir & Weir Writings

Name	Name
Address	Address
City	City
State Zip	State Zip